To Doreen & Davie   Bobby & Kirsty.

'Good Luck in your new home!

lots of love fae
   Magnus, Teresa, Tanya, george, Ian, James,
                   Robbie, Emma & Katie x

August 2006.

sunday lunch

AND OTHER RECIPES FROM THE **f** WORD

sunday lunch

AND OTHER RECIPES FROM THE f WORD

with Mark Sargeant
and Emily Quah

photographs by Jill Mead

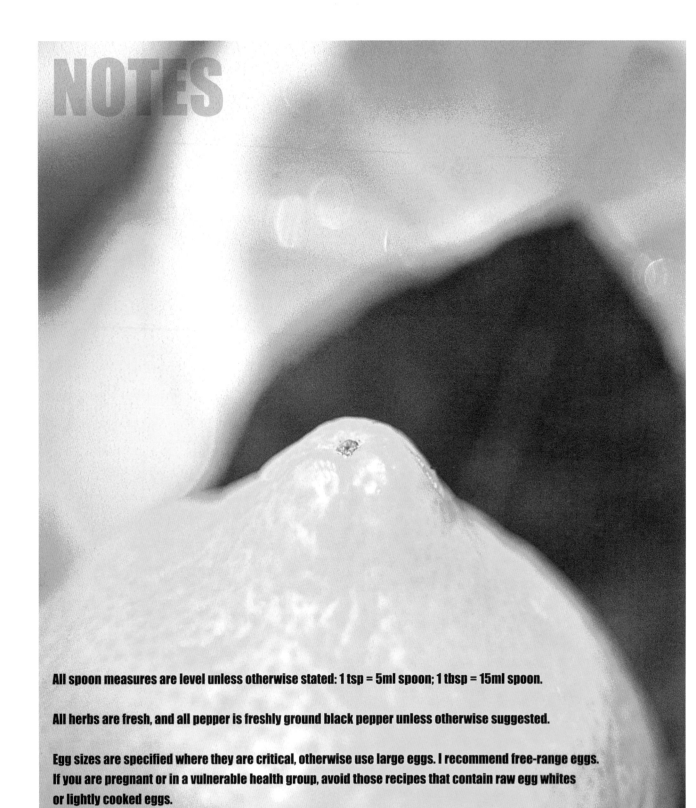

NOTES

All spoon measures are level unless otherwise stated: 1 tsp = 5ml spoon; 1 tbsp = 15ml spoon.

All herbs are fresh, and all pepper is freshly ground black pepper unless otherwise suggested.

Egg sizes are specified where they are critical, otherwise use large eggs. I recommend free-range eggs.
If you are pregnant or in a vulnerable health group, avoid those recipes that contain raw egg whites
or lightly cooked eggs.

My oven timings are for fan-assisted ovens. If you are using a conventional oven increase the
temperature by 10–15°C (½ Gas Mark). Individual ovens can deviate by as much as 10°C from the
setting, either way. Get to know your oven and use an oven thermometer to check its accuracy.
My timings are provided as guidelines, with a description of colour or texture where appropriate.

CONTENTS

RECIPE LIST

Accompaniments

Asparagus with herb butter (p43)

Courgettes provençale (p15)

Sautéed Brussels sprouts with toasted almonds (p211)

Brussels sprouts gratinée (p36)

Broccoli with red onions, capers & almonds (p223)

Sprouting broccoli with pine nuts & sesame seeds (p177)

Sautéed cabbage with caramelised onions (p71)

Creamed cabbage & celeriac with pancetta (p153)

Buttered Savoy cabbage (p33)

Savoy cabbage with marjoram (p36)

Stir-fried bok choy (p117)

Braised red cabbage (p37)

Sautéed red chard with garlic (p191)

Cavolo nero with garlic & chilli (p176)

Braised kale with pancetta (p176)

Sautéed spinach with nutmeg (p176)

Spinach with garlic, chilli & pine nuts (p107)

Watercress & spinach purée (p177)

Wilted baby gem lettuce (p183)

Braised cos lettuce (p127)

Bubble & squeak (p36)

Spiced aubergine purée (p61)

Braised leeks (p120)

Creamed leeks (p127)

Caramelised shallots with thyme (p121)

Balsamic roasted red onions (p107)

Stuffed onions (p120)

Deep-fried onion rings (p121)

Red onion & sweet potato rösti (p74)

Honey glazed carrots (p213)

Pan-roasted carrots with gremolata (p194)

Glazed carrots with thyme & garlic (p71)

Glazed carrots with rosemary (p195)

Spiced carrots with star anise (p195)

Carrot purée (p194)

Glazed parsnips (p213)

Minted new potatoes (p191)

Pommes purée (p43)

Mustard mash (p33)

Champ with spring onions & broad beans (p75)

Duchess potatoes (p74)

Sautéed potatoes with thyme & garlic (p183)

Sautéed potatoes with paprika (p75)

Oven chips (p134)

Golden roasted potatoes (p211)

Roast potatoes with garlic & rosemary (p71)

Roast Charlotte potatoes with chorizo (p75)

Potatoes boulangère (p14)

Gratin dauphinoise (p153)

Coconut rice (p117)

Green bean, spinach & red onion salad (p91)

Cos, red onion & asparagus salad (p243)

Carrot, beetroot & orange salad (p194)

Red cabbage slaw (p37)

Spring onion & wild rice salad (p121)

New potato salad (p91)

Desserts

White chocolate panacotta with Champagne granita (p224)

Iced berries with white chocolate sauce (p165)

Poached apricots with vanilla custard (p233)

Citrus jelly with passion fruit coulis (p25)

Lemon posset (p175)

Knickerbocker glory (p35)

Blueberry & redcurrant Eton mess (p93)

Summer pudding (p63)

Rhubarb crème brûlée (p109)

Coffee & chocolate mousse cups (p147)

Ginger chocolate cheesecake (p100)

Gordon's trifle (p185)

Lemon tart (p137)

Cardamom custard tart (p119)

Fig & frangipane tart (p154)

Apple tarte fine with rum & raisin ice cream (p192)

Hugh's chestnut & chocolate truffle cake (p214)

Cardamom & rosewater fragrant rice (p53)

Passion fruit & banana soufflé (p245)

Roasted rhubarb crumble (p129)

Helen's eve's pudding (p73)

Strawberry, peach & ginger crumble (p203)

Cherry clafoutis (p83)

Gordon's apple pudding (p45)

Baguette & butter pudding (p17)

INTRODUCTION

I decided to launch my Sunday lunch campaign because I was shocked to discover how many families never sit down to eat together. You don't necessarily have to be a big family in order to share food around a table and enjoy each other's company. And it doesn't have to be a Sunday, it can be a Saturday, it can be a Friday, any time of any day when families and friends can bond, sharing laughter as well as sadness. It's also an opportunity for individuals, especially children, to gain in confidence. The spine of my campaign is to reignite and reintroduce that special time of the week.

When I was growing up in Stratford-upon-Avon, Sunday lunch was a religion. It didn't matter what else was happening, we always had a family meal. Invariably, it was a big main meal followed by the most amazing apple pie, or something like a trifle. And no one was allowed to leave the table until everyone had finished.

No matter how busy our current lifestyles are, or what is going on outside, family meals are really important. At home, Tana and I make sure we eat together as a family at least three times a week – usually Friday teatime, Saturday lunchtime and, of course, Sunday lunch. Saturday lunches are always very casual. Sunday lunch has forever been routine. Even when the children were tiny and eating pureés, we still ate together. Like many other families with young children, we tend to rotate roast chicken, lamb, beef etc., introducing new flavours and different vegetables each week. As tastes broaden, so do the meals we share together.

The most exciting thing about this book is the way it is presented, with the recipes arranged as menus. Of course, these are entirely flexible – you can skip the starter if you like, or mix and match starters and desserts with main courses. But the menus take the effort out of planning a balanced three-course meal and they guide you on scheduling your time to ensure a stress-free meal.

I am determined to revive Sunday lunch, to take the intimidation out of cooking and get families back around the table. Join me and help to make my Sunday lunch campaign work.

Gordon Ramsay.

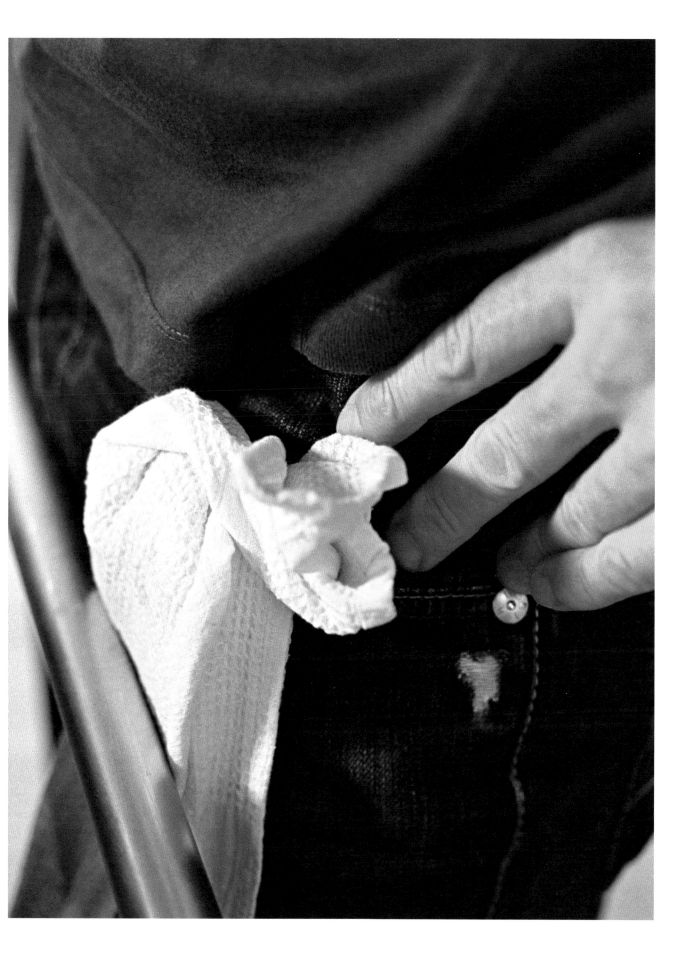

01 Mediterranean flavours

Sweet, succulent lamb in a fragrant herb coating with rustic vegetables and a pudding with a French twist to follow... divine. I love the scallop starter too, but for an easy option you could simply hand round bowls of little Niçoise olives and toast fingers spread with tapenade. This menu serves 4.

Pan-roasted scallops with cauliflower purée
Herb-crusted rack of lamb
   + Potatoes boulangère
   + Courgettes provençale
Baguette & butter pudding

planning your menu

A FEW DAYS AHEAD...
• Order the rack of lamb from your butcher and the scallops from the fish-monger (arranging to collect a day ahead, or get the shellfish on the day if possible).

SEVERAL HOURS IN ADVANCE...
• Make the baguette & butter pudding and leave to soak, ready to apply the sugar topping and cook later.
• For the starter, clean scallops and chill. Prepare the caper dressing and vinaigrette.
• Make the herb crust for the lamb; score the meat and return to the fridge.
• Prepare the potatoes boulangère and set aside, ready to cook.

TWO HOURS AHEAD...
• Bring the meat to room temperature.
• Prepare the ingredients for the courgettes provençale, ready to cook.
• Make the cauliflower purée for the starter and set aside.

ABOUT 30 MINUTES AHEAD...
• Take the scallops out of the fridge.
• Bake the potatoes boulangère.
• Sear the lamb, apply the herb crust and finish cooking in the oven.
• Bake the pudding (in a second oven if you have one, or on a low oven shelf below the lamb while it is cooking).

JUST BEFORE SERVING...
• Warm the cauliflower purée through, pan-fry the scallops and assemble the starter.
• Rest the meat while you eat the starter.
• Cook the courgettes provençale, carve the lamb and serve with the potatoes.
• Leave the pudding to rest while you eat the main course.

PAN-ROASTED SCALLOPS WITH CAULIFLOWER PUREE

" This is a great starter that we keep coming back to, because the combination of flavours is truly outstanding. Sweet scallops served on a creamy cauliflower purée and topped with a sweet and salty caper dressing... simply divine. "

4 servings

100g sultanas
100g capers in brine, rinsed and drained
12–16 large scallops, shelled and
  cleaned
1 tsp mild curry powder
sea salt and freshly ground black pepper
olive oil, for cooking

VINAIGRETTE:
1 tbsp sherry vinegar
3 tbsp olive oil

CAULIFLOWER PUREE:
½ head of cauliflower, about 350g,
  trimmed
30g butter
1–2 tbsp milk
100ml single cream

TIP To ensure that the scallops are cooked evenly, place them in a ring in the pan, arranging them in a clockwise order. A minute later, turn them over starting with the first scallop at the 12 o'clock position. This way, all the scallops should be cooked evenly.

Put the sultanas, capers and 100ml water into a small pan and bring to the boil. Tip into a food processor and whiz to a purée. For a smoother result, pass the mixture through a fine sieve.

For the vinaigrette, whisk the sherry vinegar and olive oil together to emulsify and season with salt and pepper to taste. Set aside.

For the purée, cut the cauliflower into florets. Melt the butter in a saucepan, add the cauliflower florets and sauté for about 3–4 minutes. Add a little milk, cover and sweat for 2–3 minutes, then pour in the cream and return to a gentle boil. Partially cover and cook for a few more minutes until the florets are soft. Season well.

Tip the cauliflower and cream into a food processor and blend for a few minutes until smooth, scraping down the sides of the processor a few times. (It is much easier to do this while the mixture is still hot.)

Lightly sprinkle both sides of the scallops with the curry powder and seasoning. Heat a little olive oil in a large non-stick frying pan. Add the scallops and cook for just a minute on each side, turning them in the order they were put in. They should be nicely brown on both sides and feel springy when pressed. Remove from the pan to a warm plate and leave to rest for a minute.

Slice each scallop in half horizontally and season well. Put 6–7 little spoonfuls of the cauliflower purée on each plate and top each with a scallop half. Drizzle with the caper dressing and vinaigrette and serve immediately.

13

HERB-CRUSTED RACK OF LAMB

" At the restaurant, our racks of lamb arrive French trimmed and ready to go. Your local butcher may supply you with a West Country rack, which is usually larger with more meat and fat extending to the top of the bones. Trim off the excess fat but don't waste the extra meat. You will need to cook these racks for an extra 5–10 minutes. "

4 servings

**2 large racks of lamb, cut in half
(3–4 bones in each portion)
olive oil, for cooking
sea salt and freshly ground black pepper
2 tbsp English mustard**

**HERB CRUST:
4 slices of day-old bread, crusts removed
large handful of parsley
small handful of coriander
small bunch of thyme
few rosemary sprigs
50g Parmesan, freshly grated**

Heat the oven to 200°C/Gas 6. Score the lamb fat in a criss-cross pattern and season well. Seal the racks in a hot ovenproof pan with a little olive oil until golden brown, about 4 minutes each side. Transfer the pan to the oven for 10–15 minutes to finish cooking the lamb. It should feel springy when pressed. Leave to rest while you prepare the herb crust.

Tear the bread into pieces and put into a food processor. Roughly chop the herb leaves and add to the processor with the Parmesan and a little seasoning. Whiz to fine crumbs, which will take on a bright green colour. Brush the lamb with mustard and coat with the herb crust, patting it on firmly. Return the lamb to the pan and warm through in the oven for 5 minutes.

Slice the lamb into individual chops and serve three per person, with the Pommes boulangère and Courgettes provençale.

Pommes boulangère

Heat the oven to 200°C/Gas 6. Bring the stock to the boil with the thyme, rosemary and 3 smashed garlic cloves added. Turn off the heat and leave to infuse for 20 minutes, then strain. Finely chop the other garlic cloves. Sauté the onions and chopped garlic in a little olive oil until softened, about 6–8 minutes. Meanwhile, peel the potatoes and finely slice, using a mandolin if possible.

Layer the potatoes and onions in a large shallow ovenproof dish, seasoning well as you do so and finishing with a layer of potatoes. Pour in enough stock to comes two-thirds up the side of the dish (you may not need all of it). Press down on the potatoes and finally drizzle a little olive oil on top. Bake for about 35–40 minutes until golden brown on top and the potatoes are tender when pierced.

4 servings

**400ml chicken stock (see page 246)
1 thyme sprig
2 rosemary sprigs
5 garlic cloves, peeled
2 large onions, peeled and sliced
a little olive oil, for cooking
4 large waxy potatoes, such as
Desirée or Charlotte
sea salt and freshly ground
black pepper**

Courgettes provençale

4 servings

4 large courgettes
olive oil, for cooking
1 rosemary sprig, leaves finely chopped
sea salt and freshly ground black pepper
2 tbsp balsamic vinegar
175g cherry tomatoes, halved
few basil sprigs, leaves torn

Cut the courgettes on the diagonal into 1cm thick slices. Heat a little olive oil in a large sauté pan. Add the courgettes with the chopped rosemary and sauté for a minute, seasoning well and adding a dash of balsamic vinegar. Tip in the cherry tomatoes and cook for 2–3 minutes, adding a little more olive oil, seasoning and vinegar. Allow to cook until the courgettes and tomatoes have just begun to soften. Toss in the basil leaves, check the seasoning and serve immediately.

BAGUETTE & BUTTER PUDDING

" This pudding has become a firm favourite on our restaurant menus. The thin pillowy texture of the baguette is perfect for soaking up the creamy custard, which is flavoured with Cointreau though you can, of course, try different liqueurs. "

4–6 servings

50g unsalted butter, softened

4 tbsp apricot jam

1 large French baguette, about 200g, thinly sliced

60g sultanas or dried cranberries (or a mixture of both)

2 large eggs

2 large egg yolks

40g caster sugar

300ml double cream

300ml milk

4 tbsp Cointreau, or more to taste

demerara sugar, to sprinkle

TO SERVE:

120ml pouring cream

a little Cointreau (optional)

TIP This pudding is cooked in a bain-marie (water bath) to temper the oven heat. This prevents the custard from overheating, which can result in curdling.

Use a large knob of the butter to grease the sides of a 1.5 litre shallow ovenproof dish. Spread 1 tbsp of the jam in the bottom of the dish. Butter the bread slices and arrange them in the dish in overlapping layers, sprinkling the dried fruit between.

Beat the eggs, egg yolks and caster sugar together in a large bowl until creamy, then beat in the cream, milk and Cointreau. Slowly pour this mixture over the bread. Press the bread slices down gently with your fingers so they are completely submerged. Leave to stand for about 20 minutes to allow the bread to soak up the custard. Preheat the oven to 180°C/Gas 4.

Stand the dish in a roasting tin and surround with boiling water to come halfway up the sides of the dish. Sprinkle the demerara sugar evenly over the top of the pudding and bake in the oven for 40–50 minutes until golden.

As soon as the pudding is ready, warm the remaining apricot jam with 1 tbsp water until runny. Dab this glaze over the surface of the pudding with a pastry brush and leave to stand for 15 minutes before serving. The custard will continue to cook and firm up during this time. Serve warm with a drizzle of cream, flavoured with a little Cointreau if you like.

02 Spring greens

Fresh spring flavours sing out from this colourful menu. Gooseberry sauce and spring greens are the perfect foil for rich duck breasts and the prepare-ahead dessert is truly refreshing. Vary the topping for the little tarts, making them as simple as you like. This menu serves 6.

Artichoke, asparagus, tomato & onion tart
Duck breast with spring greens & gooseberry sauce
Citrus jelly with passion fruit coulis

planning your menu

THE DAY BEFORE...
• Make the citrus jelly and the passion fruit coulis and refrigerate.

SEVERAL HOURS IN ADVANCE...
• For the starter, make the onion purée. Shape and bake the pastry bases.

AN HOUR IN ADVANCE...
• Prepare the spice mix, score the duck fat and coat with the spice. Set aside at room temperature.
• For the tarts, blanch the asparagus, boil the quail's eggs and prepare the other ingredients ready to assemble.
• Make the gooseberry sauce.
• Prepare the spring greens ready to cook.

JUST BEFORE SERVING...
• Assemble the starter.
• Pan-fry the duck breasts and put into the oven to finish cooking while you eat your starter.
• Rest the duck while you wilt the spring greens and reheat the sauce.
• Slice the duck and serve with the sauce.
• Turn out the jelly, slice and serve with the coulis.

ARTICHOKE, ASPARAGUS, TOMATO & ONION TART

"My children call these gorgeous little tarts 'mini pizzas'. Indeed, you can adapt the toppings as you like. Semi-dried tomatoes are a good alternative to fresh ones and to save time, you could use ready-made tapenade in place of the onion purée."

6 servings

ONION PUREE:
olive oil, for cooking
6 onions, peeled and finely chopped
sea salt and freshly ground black pepper
4 tbsp single cream

TART:
500g ready-made puff pastry
flour, to dust
150g asparagus tips
12 quail's eggs
150g ready-cooked artichoke hearts, cut into wedges
150g cherry tomatoes, halved
½ small red onion, peeled and finely sliced
small handful of chives, chopped
3–4 tbsp Classic vinaigrette (see page 247)
few rocket leaves, to garnish

TIP Lightly roll the boiled quail's eggs on the work surface to gently crush the shells, making them easier to peel.

For the onion purée, heat a little olive oil in a pan, add the onions and season well. Cover and cook over a low heat, stirring occasionally, for 10–15 minutes until the onions are very soft. Meanwhile, heat the oven to 200°C/Gas 6.

Roll out the pastry thinly on a lightly floured surface and cut out 6 discs, using a 13–15cm plate or saucer as a guide. Lay the pastry discs on a large baking sheet and prick all over with a skewer. Place another heavy baking sheet on top of the pastry discs to weigh them down. Bake for 15 minutes until brown and crisp. Transfer to a wire rack to cool.

Add the cream to the onions and bring to a simmer. Tip the mixture into a blender or food processor and whiz to a fine paste. For a very smooth purée, push the onion paste through a sieve. Leave to cool.

Blanch the asparagus tips in a pan of boiling salted water for 2 minutes until tender. Remove with tongs and refresh in a bowl of iced water, then drain and tip into a large bowl.

Add the quail's eggs to the boiling water in the pan carefully, and cook for 2 minutes, 10 seconds. This will leave the eggs with runny yolks. Refresh under cold running water and peel off the shells.

Add the artichokes, tomatoes, red onion and chives to the asparagus, drizzle with the vinaigrette and toss to mix.

Spoon a little onion purée over the centre of the pastry discs and pile the vegetables on top. Halve the quail's eggs and arrange on the vegetables. Scatter a few rocket leaves over, sprinkle with a little salt and pepper and serve.

DUCK BREAST
WITH SPRING GREENS & GOOSEBERRY SAUCE

" Tart fruits such as gooseberries go really well with duck, because they cut through the richness of the meat. The spring greens add a touch of lightness to this meal. "

6 servings

3 tbsp Szechwan peppercorns
sea salt and freshly ground black pepper
6 duck breasts with skin, about 175g each
300ml Sugar syrup (see page 248)
150g gooseberries
150ml dry red wine
150ml brown Chicken (or duck) stock
   (see page 246)
3 tbsp gooseberry conserve or honey
few knobs of butter
400g spring greens, cored and finely
   shredded

TIP If you prefer a smooth sauce, press the gooseberries through a fine sieve before adding them to the sauce.

Toast the peppercorns in a dry pan until fragrant, then tip into a pestle and mortar and add a little salt and pepper. Lightly crush the peppercorn mix. Score the skin of the duck breasts in a criss-cross pattern, then coat with the spice mixture.

Place the duck breasts, skin side down, in a dry ovenproof pan and cook over a very low heat to render down most of the fat. This may take 10–15 minutes. Heat the oven to 200°C/Gas 6.

Heat the sugar syrup in a pan, meanwhile. Add the gooseberries and gently poach for 2–3 minutes. Leave them to cool in the sugar syrup.

For the sauce, boil the red wine in a pan for 7–8 minutes until reduced by half. Pour in the stock and again, reduce by half.

Turn up the heat under the duck breasts and fry until the skin is crisp. Turn them over and seal the other side for 1–2 minutes. Transfer the pan to the hot oven and cook for 8–10 minutes for medium-rare duck – it should be slightly springy when pressed.

In the meantime, stir the gooseberry conserve into the sauce and add a knob of butter for shine. Drain the gooseberries, add them to the sauce and warm through. Taste and adjust the seasoning.

When ready, rest the duck on a warm plate for 10 minutes. Wilt the spring greens with a couple of knobs of butter in a hot pan. Season well, then divide among warm serving plates. Thickly slice the duck breasts on the diagonal and fan out on top of the spring greens. Spoon the sauce over and around to serve.

CITRUS JELLY WITH PASSION FRUIT COULIS

" This is a stunning dessert, worth the little extra time and patience required. It is also fat free, so perfect for anyone on a low-fat diet. You can set the jelly in a loaf tin or terrine and slice it to serve, or in individual moulds. We use triangular moulds in the restaurants, but you could use any shape. "

6–8 servings

2 pink grapefruit
2 white grapefruit
4 large seedless oranges
5 gelatine leaves
200ml Sugar syrup (see page 248)

PASSION FRUIT COULIS:
2 ripe passion fruit
200ml Sugar syrup (see page 248)

Slice off the tops and bottoms off the grapefruit and oranges, using a sharp, serrated knife, then cut away the remaining peel, removing the pith too. Segment the fruit by cutting the segments free from the membranes, holding the fruit over a sieve set on a bowl to catch the juice. Squeeze out the excess juice from the core of each fruit before discarding. Reserve the juice. Remove any membrane or pips left on the segments.

Lay the fruit segments on a tray lined with a clean tea towel and chill for an hour. This is to dry the fruit and prevent any excess juice from diluting the jelly as it sets.

Measure the citrus juice collected; you need 200ml. Soak the gelatine leaves in a bowl of cold water. Bring the sugar syrup to the boil in a pan, then remove from the heat. Squeeze out excess water from the gelatine leaves and add them to the hot syrup. Stir until the gelatine has dissolved, then mix with the citrus juice.

Arrange the grapefruit and orange segments randomly in a 1kg loaf tin or terrine. Pour the jelly mixture over the fruit segments and chill overnight until the jelly is set.

For the coulis, simply halve the passion fruit and spoon the juice and seeds into the sugar syrup. Chill until needed.

To unmould the jelly, dip the tin in hot water for 2 seconds, then invert on to a board and give the tin a gentle shake to release the jelly. Cut into slices with a sharp knife and lift on to serving plates. Serve with a drizzle of passion fruit coulis.

"Sunday lunch is the perfect excuse to get people together. It doesn't just have to be the immediate family – it can be friends, neighbours, relatives – remember Auntie Joan? Join me in getting Sunday lunch back on the menu."

03 Winter casserole

Slow-cooked beef in red wine followed by an all-time favourite dessert... this is comfort food at its best. An ideal Sunday lunch, especially if you're planning to go out in the morning, as the casserole tastes even better made a day ahead. This menu serves 6.

Lamb's lettuce & celery salad with Fourme d'Ambert

Beef casserole
+ Buttered Savoy cabbage
+ Mustard mash

Knickerbocker glory

planning your menu

THE DAY BEFORE...
• Make the casserole and refrigerate overnight (or make it early on the day).
• Make the jelly for the dessert and chill to set.

AN HOUR OR TWO AHEAD...
• Take the casserole out of the fridge to bring to room temperature.
• Peel the potatoes for the mash and immerse in cold water.
• Shred, blanch and refresh the cabbage.
• Prepare the ingredients for the salad ready to assemble.

ABOUT 30 MINUTES IN ADVANCE...
• Reheat the casserole in a low oven.
• For the dessert, prepare the fruit, chop the jelly and crush the amaretti. Set aside, ready to assemble.
• Cook the potatoes and prepare the mash; keep warm.

JUST BEFORE SERVING...
• Assemble the starter and serve.
• Sauté the cabbage, then serve the main course.
• Assemble the knickerbocker glories just before serving.

LAMB'S LETTUCE & CELERY SALAD WITH FOURME D'AMBERT

" Comprising three simple ingredients, this is a wonderfully light, refreshing salad. Fourme d'Ambert is one of my favourite cheeses. It is a mild blue from the Loire and Puy-de-Dôme regions and is regarded as one of the oldest of all French cheeses. During the maturing process, it is washed or injected with local white wine, giving the salty cheese a slightly sweet, nutty flavour and a lovely, creamy texture. You can also serve this salad as a light lunch, with plenty of warm, crusty bread. "

6 servings

5 celery stalks, trimmed
200g lamb's lettuce
150g Fourme d'Ambert
6 tbsp Classic vinaigrette (see page 247)
sea salt and freshly ground black pepper
handful of crushed, toasted walnuts
  (optional)

Finely chop the celery and put it into a large salad bowl. Twist off any thick root ends from the lamb's lettuce, then add to the celery. Crumble half the cheese into the bowl, then drizzle with 3–4 tbsp of the vinaigrette and toss to mix.

Pile the salad on to individual plates, crumble over the remaining cheese and sprinkle with salt and pepper. For added texture, scatter over a handful of crushed walnuts. Drizzle over the remaining vinaigrette and serve.

TIP If you can't buy Fourme d'Ambert from your local cheese shop, then substitute Gorgonzola, Bleu d'Auvergne or any mild, crumbly blue cheese.

BEEF CASSEROLE

> " This casserole is the perfect winter warmer. Braising beef is slowly cooked with herbs and vegetables in red wine, which gives the stew a depth of colour and a wonderful rich flavour. Flavoured mash and sautéed cabbage are ideal accompaniments. "

6 servings

800g braising beef
3 tbsp plain flour
sea salt and freshly ground black pepper
olive oil, for cooking
200g smoked bacon lardons
2 medium carrots, peeled
1 small celeriac, about 700g, peeled
150g pearl onions (or baby shallots),
   peeled
few thyme sprigs
2 bay leaves
250g chestnut mushrooms, trimmed
   halved if large
1 tsp tomato purée
500ml red wine
300ml beef or brown Chicken stock
   (see page 246)
handful of flat leaf parsley, chopped

Heat the oven to 150°C/Gas 2. Cut the beef into bite-sized chunks. Season the flour with salt and pepper and toss the meat in the flour to coat. Heat a little olive oil in a large cast-iron casserole over a medium heat. Sear the beef briefly in two or three batches until browned all over, then transfer to a plate and set aside.

Add the lardons to the casserole and fry gently until lightly golden, adding a little olive oil if necessary. Meanwhile, cut the carrots and celeriac into 2cm cubes. Tip them into the pan with the whole onions, thyme and bay leaves and stir over a medium heat for 5 minutes until the vegetables begin to soften. Stir in the mushrooms and tomato purée and sauté for another 2–3 minutes.

Pour in the red wine and scrape the bottom of the pan with a wooden spoon to deglaze. Add the stock and bring the liquid to the boil, then lower the heat and simmer for a few minutes. Return the beef to the casserole and stir to immerse the meat in the liquid completely. Put the lid on the casserole and cook in the oven for 2½ hours or until the beef is very tender.

Check the seasoning, then scatter the chopped parsley over the stew. Serve with the accompaniments.

Buttered Savoy cabbage

Finely slice the cabbage and blanch in a pan of
boiling salted water for 2 minutes. Drain, and if not serving immediately, refresh under cold running water. Drain well again. Just before serving, melt the butter in a wide, heavy-based pan, add the blanched cabbage and season well with salt and pepper. Toss over a medium heat for 1–2 minutes until the cabbage is just tender. Serve at once.

6 servings

1 Savoy cabbage, trimmed
sea salt and freshly ground black pepper
25g unsalted butter

Mustard mash

6 servings

1 kg floury potatoes, such as Desirée or King Edward
sea salt and freshly ground black pepper
150ml double cream
85g butter, cut into cubes
2 tbsp wholegrain mustard
1–2 tbsp Dijon mustard

Peel the potatoes and cut into large, even-sized
chunks. Cook in boiling salted water for 12–15 minutes until tender. Drain well, then return to the pan and dry out for 1–2 minutes over a medium heat. Mash the potatoes well, preferably using a potato ricer back into the pan. For a very smooth result, push the mashed potato through a fine sieve. Gently heat the cream and slowly stir into the mashed potato. Season well. Cook gently for 5 minutes, then gradually beat in the butter, a cube at a time. Finally stir in the mustards and season with salt and pepper to taste. Serve warm.

KNICKERBOCKER GLORY

"Admittedly a little 'over-the-top', this tempting dessert is an adult-version of a childhood treat. To accommodate children, cook the cherries in sugar syrup instead of kirsch. If you prefer, melt the chocolate buttons and pour the warm chocolate sauce over the ice cream, just before serving. Provide thin, long-handled serving spoons so everyone can delve down through the layers."

6 servings

140g packet strawberry jelly
300g ripe cherries, pitted
75ml kirsch
50g caster sugar
1 small ripe mango
100g strawberries, hulled
2 clementines
500ml good-quality vanilla ice cream
50g amaretti biscuits
40g chocolate buttons

Break the jelly into small pieces and put into a bowl. Pour on 3 tbsp boiling water and microwave on high for 1–1½ minutes. Stir until completely dissolved, then mix in 400ml cold water. Pour the jelly into a shallow bowl or loaf tin and chill overnight to set.

Place the cherries in a non-stick pan, sprinkle with the kirsch and sugar and cook over a high heat for 1–2 minutes until the cherries are soft but still holding their shape. Remove from the heat and leave to cool.

Put six tall glasses into the refrigerator to chill, ready for serving.

Peel the mango and cut the flesh away from the stone, then chop into 1cm cubes. Quarter or slice the strawberries depending on size. Peel the clementines and slice them horizontally into thin rounds.

Unmould the jelly on to a board and roughly chop into small pieces. Lightly crush the amaretti biscuits in a bowl with the end of a rolling pin.

To assemble, layer the cherries, mango, clementines, chopped jelly, ice cream, strawberries and chocolate buttons in the chilled glasses. Top with a final scoop of ice cream and sprinkle with the crushed amaretti biscuits. Serve immediately.

5 ways with...CABBAGE

Savoy cabbage with marjoram
Serves 4–6

Trim and finely shred 1 small Savoy cabbage. Blanch in a pan of boiling salted water for 2–3 minutes until tender; drain well. Melt 50g butter in a wide heavy-based pan. Toss in the cabbage and season well. Add the chopped leaves from a few marjoram sprigs, fold through and serve warm. Lovely with chicken or fish dishes.

Bubble & squeak
Serves 4

Trim and finely shred ½ Savoy cabbage. Blanch in a pan of boiling salted water for 2–3 minutes until tender; drain well. Mix the blanched cabbage with 500g cooked mashed potatoes and season generously with salt and pepper. With lightly floured hands, shape the potato and cabbage mixture into individual patties. Heat 25g butter and 2 tbsp olive oil in a heavy-based frying pan and fry the patties over a low heat for several minutes until a crust forms on the bottom. Turn over and cook the other side until golden brown and crisp. Serve warm with Sunday lunch roasts.

Brussels sprouts gratinée
Serves 6

Cook 750g trimmed Brussels sprouts in boiling salted water for 6–8 minutes until just tender. Drain and refresh under cold running water, then cut in half. Melt 20g butter in a saucepan and stir in 20g plain flour. Cook, stirring, for 1–2 minutes over a low heat. Add a pinch of dry English mustard, a pinch of cayenne and some salt and pepper. Gradually whisk in 300ml milk, a little at a time, to make a smooth sauce. Allow to simmer, stirring frequently, until the sauce thickens and coats the back of a wooden spoon. Over a very low heat, stir in 70g grated mature Cheddar until melted.
When ready to serve, toss the Brussels sprouts with the cheese sauce, place in a large gratin dish (or two smaller ones) and sprinkle with some more grated cheese. Place under a hot grill for a few minutes until the cheese topping is bubbling and golden brown, then serve. A good accompaniment to roast chicken or a fish pie.

Braised red cabbage
Serves 4–6

Heat the oven to 180°C/Gas 4. Quarter, core and finely shred 1 red cabbage and place in a large ovenproof casserole with 200ml clear malt vinegar, 150g light brown sugar and 150g melted unsalted butter. Season generously with salt and pepper and stir well. Cook in the oven for 1½–1¾ hours, stirring every 30 minutes to prevent the top from drying out. If there is still a fair amount of liquid, strain it off and boil until reduced to a syrupy sauce, then pour back over the cabbage and toss to coat. Superb with game birds, such as wild pigeon, or duck.

Red cabbage slaw
Serves 6

Quarter, core and finely shred 1 red cabbage and place in a large salad bowl. Grate 2 peeled carrots and 2 peeled, cored crisp apples (such as Granny Smiths) and add them to the cabbage with a squeeze of lemon juice, 50g toasted walnut pieces and 30g golden sultanas or raisins. Toss well to mix.

For the dressing, beat together 120ml Mayonnaise (see page 247), 4 tbsp Greek yogurt and 1 tbsp orange juice in a bowl. Season with salt and pepper to taste and stir in 2 tbsp chopped chives. Spoon the dressing over the salad and toss until well coated. Cover and chill for about half an hour. Toss the salad again just before serving. Ideal with a barbecue or *al fresco* meal.

04 Chicken chic

I love the subtle flavours running through this menu – a velvety soup of white beans, a mushroom-infused sauce to enhance chicken and a comforting apple sponge to finish. For a lighter dessert, you could omit the sponge and simply serve the caramelised apples with crème anglaise. This menu serves 4.

Haricot soup with tiger prawns
Chicken breast with a morel velouté
+ Pommes purée
+ Asparagus with herb butter
Gordon's apple pudding

planning your menu

THE DAY BEFORE...
• For the soup, cook the haricot beans, purée and refrigerate.
• Prepare the chicken crowns and chill.
• Make the herb butter for the asparagus and chill.

SEVERAL HOURS IN ADVANCE...
• Take the chicken (and the butter and eggs for the pudding) out of the fridge.
• Make the morel velouté.
• Soak the sultanas and caramelise the apples for the pudding. Leave to cool.

TWO HOURS AHEAD...
• Make the pommes purée.
• Blanch the prawns for the soup.
• Prepare the flavoured crème fraîche and refrigerate.
• Poach the chicken crowns and allow to rest; don't chill.

FROM AN HOUR AHEAD...
• Carve out the chicken breasts.
• Make and bake the apple pudding.
• Prepare the asparagus ready for cooking.

JUST BEFORE SERVING...
• Reheat the bean purée and make the soup (ready to whisk in the butter at the last minute). Sauté the prawns.
• Pan-fry the chicken breasts and reheat the velouté.
• Finish the soup and rest the chicken while you have the starter.
• Reheat the pommes purée adding a few extra knobs of butter, cook the asparagus and serve the main course.
• Leave the pudding at room temperature to cool slightly while you eat the main course, then serve with the crème fraîche.

HARICOT SOUP WITH TIGER PRAWNS

" Puréed haricot beans provide a velvety background to tiger prawns – a concept we call *terre et mer*, which combines the flavours of the land and sea. In a dish like this, we generally use chicken stock as the base for the soup, as fish stock would overpower the distinctive but delicate flavour of the beans. "

4 servings

250g dried haricot beans, soaked overnight
1 small onion, peeled and halved
1 carrot, peeled and halved
1 bouquet garni (thyme, bay leaf and parsley tied together)
800ml Court bouillon (see page 247)
18 tiger prawns, peeled and deveined
300ml Chicken (or vegetable) stock (see page 246)
150ml double cream
sea salt and freshly ground black pepper
30g cold butter, cut into cubes, plus a few knobs for frying
handful of chives, finely chopped
olive oil, to drizzle

Drain the haricot beans and place
in a saucepan. Add the onion, carrot and bouquet garni and cover with cold water. Bring to the boil and boil steadily for 10 minutes, then lower the heat to a simmer. Partially cover the pan and cook for 1½–2 hours until the beans are soft, stirring occasionally and topping up with boiling water if they appear dry. Drain the beans and discard the onion, carrot and bouquet garni. Scoop out about 4 tbsp beans and set aside for the garnish.

Whiz the beans in a blender to a smooth purée,
adding a touch of boiling water if necessary (to get the blades moving) and scraping down the sides a couple of times. For a really smooth soup, push the purée through a fine sieve.

Bring the court bouillon to the boil
in a pan, add the prawns and blanch for 30 seconds, then drain and refresh under cold running water. Cut each prawn into two or three bite-sized pieces if you like.

Pour the bean purée into a pan and
reheat gently, then whisk in the stock and cream and season with salt and pepper to taste. Whisk in the cold butter, a piece at a time, using a hand-held stick blender if you like – to froth up the soup.

Sauté the prawns and reserved beans with a
few knobs of butter to heat through. Season well, add the chives and toss through. Pile into the centre of warm bowls, pour the soup around them and serve, drizzled with a little olive oil.

CHICKEN BREAST WITH A MOREL VELOUTE

" This is the perfect way to cook chicken breasts – gently poach them on the bone to keep the meat flavourful and succulent, then pan-fry to give them a golden, crisp skin. Dried morels lend an intense flavour to the cream sauce. "

4 servings

2 free-range chickens, about 900g–1kg each

1 head of garlic (unpeeled), halved horizontally

sea salt and freshly ground black pepper

2 tbsp chicken bouillon powder

1 tbsp black peppercorns, lightly crushed

1 tbsp coriander seeds, lightly crushed

1 thyme sprig

2 bay leaves

2 leeks, trimmed and roughly chopped

2 carrots, peeled and roughly chopped

2 celery stalks, trimmed and roughly chopped

olive oil, for cooking

few knobs of butter

MOREL VELOUTE:

10–12 dried morels

olive oil, for cooking

3 large shallots, peeled and finely sliced

1 thyme sprig

1 garlic clove, peeled and crushed

175ml dry white wine

250ml double cream

Remove the legs, wings and parson's nose from the chickens, to leave the crown of the birds. (Save the legs and wings for another dish.) Put the garlic in the cavities and season well. Soak the dried morels for the velouté in hot water for 20 minutes.

Two-thirds fill a large pan with cold water (enough to cover the chickens). Add the bouillon powder, peppercorns, coriander seeds, herbs and vegetables. Bring to the boil and simmer for 10 minutes. Add the chicken crowns and poach for 10–12 minutes or until the breasts feel firm. (Depending on the pan, you may need to poach them one at a time.) Remove from the pan and leave to rest for 5 minutes. Reserve the poaching stock.

Make the velouté in the meantime. Drain and chop the morels, reserving the liquid. Heat a little olive oil in a pan and sauté the shallots, thyme and garlic for 5–6 minutes until golden. Add the morels, a little more oil and seasoning. Cook for 5–6 minutes, then carefully pour in most of the morel soaking liquor (leaving the sediment behind). Add the wine and bubble until almost totally reduced. Add 2–3 ladlefuls of the reserved chicken poaching stock and boil for 8–10 minutes until reduced by half. Add the cream and simmer until thickened to the consistency of single cream. Pass the sauce through a sieve, pressing the mushrooms and shallots to extract as much flavour as possible. Season the sauce and return to the pan.

Carve out the breasts from the crowns carefully and pat the skin dry with kitchen paper. Heat a little olive oil in a non-stick frying pan and fry the chicken breasts until the skin is crisp and golden, 3–4 minutes each side. Add a few knobs of butter to the pan and spoon over the breasts during the final minute of cooking to keep them moist.

Rest the chicken while you reheat the velouté. Slice each chicken breast in two horizontally and season each half. Arrange on warm plates, pour the sauce around and serve with the accompaniments.

Pommes purée

Put the potatoes in a pan of cold water and bring to the boil. Lower the heat and simmer for 15–20 minutes or until they feel tender when pierced with a knife. Drain and peel while still hot (wearing rubber gloves to protect your hands from the heat if you like). Push the potatoes through a ricer or mouli. For a smoother result, press the mashed potatoes through a fine sieve with a spatula. Meanwhile, heat the milk in a pan. Toss the puréed potatoes in a dry pan to dry out a little, then beat in the butter and season with salt and pepper. Just as the milk comes to the boil, pour on to the potatoes and beat well. (If you want a thinner purée, beat in a little boiling water.) Whisk in a few extra knobs of butter for a rich, silky finish.

4 servings

1kg floury potatoes, such as King Edward or Romano, well scrubbed
100ml milk
4 tbsp butter, plus a few knobs
sea salt and freshly ground black pepper

Asparagus with herb butter

4 servings
20 asparagus spears

HERB BUTTER:
200g unsalted butter, softened
1 tsp finely chopped tarragon
1 tsp finely chopped flat leaf parsley
1 tsp finely chopped chervil
sea salt and freshly ground black pepper

For the herb butter, beat the softened butter with the chopped herbs, using a wooden spoon. Season well with salt and pepper. Spoon the herb butter on to a piece of cling film, forming a sausage shape. Roll in the cling film and wrap tightly, twisting the ends to seal. Chill until firm.

Trim the asparagus by snapping off the base of the stalks. Bring a pan of salted water to the boil and blanch the asparagus for 3–4 minutes or until tender. Meanwhile, unwrap and thinly slice the herb butter. Drain the asparagus and serve each portion topped with a few slices of herb butter.

TIP Herb butter is a simple, effective way to dress up fish, shellfish, chicken and vegetables. It can be frozen for up to a month, so make up a batch and use as required.

GORDON'S APPLE PUDDING

"This is my update on Eve's pudding, a homely baked apple pudding that's been around for ages. To enhance the flavour, I caramelise the apples with sugar and butter to give them a richness that is missing from simply stewed apples. My guests at the restaurant loved it, so I've made this generous enough for seconds!"

6 servings

50g sultanas
3 tbsp Calvados
240g unsalted butter, plus extra
  to grease
3 Braeburn or Pink Lady apples
175g demerara sugar
2 large eggs, beaten
150g self-raising flour
finely grated zest of 1 lemon
2–3 tbsp milk
30g flaked almonds (optional)
icing sugar, to dust (optional)

TO SERVE:
1 vanilla pod
200g crème fraîche

Heat the oven
to 190°C/Gas 5. Soak the sultanas in the Calvados. Lightly grease a 25cm cake tin or an ovenproof dish.

Peel, core and chop
the apples. Heat a non-stick frying pan over a medium heat, then add the apples with 15g butter and one-third of the sugar. Cook until they begin to caramelise, tossing them to ensure they colour evenly. Tip in the sultanas and Calvados and cook for a further 5–10 minutes until the apples are tender. Transfer the apple mixture to the prepared tin, spread evenly and leave to cool.

Meanwhile,
cream the remaining butter and sugar together. Beat in the eggs a little at a time, stirring in a spoonful of the flour if the mixture looks like it will split at any point. Fold in the flour and lemon zest, alternately with the milk. The mixture will be quite thick – add just enough milk to get the cake mixture to a dropping consistency.

Pour the cake mixture
over the apples and sprinkle with the flaked almonds and a dusting of icing sugar if you like. Bake for about 30–35 minutes until the top is golden brown and a skewer inserted in the middle comes out clean. Run a thin knife around the edge of the tin and leave to cool slightly.

Split the vanilla pod
and scrape out the seeds with the back of a knife, adding them to the crème fraîche. Whip until evenly blended and creamy. Serve the pudding warm, with a generous dollop of vanilla crème fraîche.

Seared beef salad with sweet mustard dressing
Pan-fried sea bass with broccoli & sorrel sauce
Cardamom & rosewater fragrant rice

A FEW DAYS AHEAD...
• Order the sea bass from the fishmonger (ask him to fillet it for you). Arrange to collect it on the day if possible, otherwise the day before.

THE DAY BEFORE...
• Make the fish velouté and keep chilled.

SEVERAL HOURS IN ADVANCE...
• Make the rice pudding and chill.
• For the starter, sear the beef and refrigerate. Make the dressing.

AN HOUR AHEAD...
• Check the fish fillets for any pin bones and bring to room temperature.
• Prepare the salad ingredients for the starter, ready to assemble.

JUST BEFORE SERVING...
• Stir the cream into the rice pudding and divide between glasses; chill.
• Toss the beef in the dressing with the herbs and plate the starter, then serve.
• Pan-fry the fish fillets, blanch the broccoli and finish the sauce, then serve.
• Top the rice puddings with a spoonful of jam and serve.

SEARED BEEF SALAD
WITH SWEET MUSTARD DRESSING

66 Inspired by steak tartare, this seared beef salad is perfect for those who are not accustomed to eating meat raw. Small cubes of beef are seared, chopped and tossed with a honey mustard dressing. The chicory acts as a refreshing palate cleanser between each bite. If making in advance, don't dress the beef until the last minute, because the vinegar in the dressing will 'cook' the beef and discolour the herbs. 99

4 servings

olive oil, for cooking and to drizzle
600g fillet of beef, cut into large 4cm chunks
sea salt and freshly ground black pepper
1 large red chicory bulb, trimmed
1 large white chicory bulb, trimmed
small bunch of mint, leaves chopped
small bunch of flat leaf parsley,
  leaves chopped

DRESSING:
1 tbsp Dijon mustard
1 tbsp cider or white wine vinegar
1 tbsp runny honey
1 tbsp soy sauce
4 tbsp olive oil

Heat a large frying pan until very hot and add a little olive oil. Season the beef with salt and pepper and sear for 3–4 minutes until browned on all sides. (You don't want to cook the beef chunks through, just sear them on the outside.) Leave to cool completely. If preparing in advance, tip into a bowl, drizzle with a little more olive oil and refrigerate.

For the dressing, mix the ingredients together and season with salt and pepper to taste. Separate the chicory leaves.

Just before serving, cut the seared beef into small cubes. Place in a bowl and toss with the dressing and chopped herbs. Divide the beef among four serving plates, centering it using a pastry ring for a professional look if you like. Garnish the plate with chicory leaves (saving the larger outer leaves for another dish). Drizzle with a little olive oil, sprinkle with sea salt and serve immediately.

" I love sea bass. Whatever you are concerned, the delicate flavour of sea bass and the excellent tip ... If you can build on it well, season and balance it ... I a minute, I don't think it needs anything else ... the simple truth is ...

4 sea bass fillets, skin on, about 175g each
olive oil, for cooking and to drizzle
sea salt and freshly ground black pepper
2 heads of broccoli, cut into florets
300ml fish Velouté (see page 247)
handful of sorrel leaves, shredded

1 Check the bass fillets for small pin bones, removing any with tweezers. Using a sharp knife, lightly score the skin at 1cm intervals. Heat a little olive oil in a large frying pan until hot. Season the fish fillets and place them in the pan, skin side down. Fry, without moving, for 2–3 minutes until the skin is crisp and the fish is cooked two-thirds of the way through. Turn the fillets and cook the other side for about 30 seconds.

2 While the fish is cooking blanch the broccoli in boiling salted water for 2 minutes and drain well. Drizzle with a little olive oil and season with salt and pepper. Keep warm.

3 Transfer the fish to a warm plate and lightly cover with a piece of foil. Pour the fish velouté into the pan and scrape up the sediment with a wooden spoon to deglaze the pan. Simmer for a few minutes, then add half of the shredded sorrel and take off the heat.

4 Divide the broccoli among warm serving plates and lay the sea bass fillets on top. Pour the sauce around the plate and garnish with the remaining shredded sorrel.

CARDAMOM & ROSEWATER FRAGRANT RICE

" Cardamom and rosewater lend a perfumed, North African flavour to this delicate chilled rice pudding. I like to top it with a spoonful of quince jam, which complements the rosewater and adds an extra touch of sweetness. If you can't find quince jam, use strawberry jam or serve the pudding on its own. "

4–6 servings

300ml double cream
8–10 cardamom pods, lightly crushed
100g caster sugar
200g pudding rice
pinch of fine sea salt
1 tsp rosewater
4–6 tsp quince or strawberry jam

Pour the cream into a small saucepan, add the cardamom and sugar and stir over a gentle heat until the sugar has dissolved. Increase the heat and as soon as the cream begins to bubble, remove the pan from the heat and set aside to infuse for an hour. Don't worry if a skin forms on the surface, it will be strained out.

Put the rice into another saucepan with 400ml water and a pinch of salt. Give it a stir, bring to the boil and then lower the heat to a simmer. Cover and cook for 15–20 minutes. Leaving the lid on, remove the pan from the heat and leave to stand for 5 minutes. Spread the rice out on a plate to cool completely.

Strain the cream through a fine sieve into a bowl, to remove the cardamom pods and seeds. Add the rosewater, then stir two-thirds of the cream into the cooled rice. (Hold back some cream to loosen the rice before serving.) Cover the bowls of rice and remaining cream with cling film and chill for at least 2 hours.

When ready to serve, stir the reserved cream into the chilled rice and spoon into individual glasses. Top each with a teaspoonful of quince jam.

NEARLY A
QUARTER OF
HOUSEHOLDS
HAVEN'T COOKED
USING FRESH
INGREDIENTS
IN THE PAST WEEK.

"Fresh means healthy.
It's not rocket science."

if you share my passion for vibrant flavours that set the tastebuds tingling, you'll love this menu. The garlicky mayonnaise is a great dip for prawns or grilled veg, such as asparagus, courgettes and peppers, if clams aren't to your taste. This menu serves 6–8.

Clams with aïoli
Roast rump of lamb with herb couscous
+ Spiced aubergine purée
Summer pudding

planning your menu

THE DAY BEFORE...
• Make the summer pudding, weigh down and chill overnight.
• Put the lamb to marinate in the fridge.
• Dégorge the aubergines, deep-fry and leave to drain overnight.

AN HOUR OR TWO IN ADVANCE...
• For the starter, clean the clams and make the aïoli.
• Prepare the aubergine purée.

ABOUT 15 MINUTES AHEAD...
• Pan-fry the lamb and put into the oven to finish cooking. Soak the couscous in boiling stock.

JUST BEFORE SERVING...
• Cook the clams.
• Add the vinaigrette and herbs to the couscous and fork through; keep warm.
• Rest the meat while you eat the starter.
• Reheat the aubergine purée, slice the lamb and serve the main course.
• Turn out the summer pudding and serve with cream.

CLAMS WITH AIOLI

For me, these are as satisfying as moules marinière. The aïoli works perfectly with the clams, which should be just cooked – there's nothing worse than overcooked, rubbery shellfish. Take the pan off the heat as soon as the clams have opened up their shells. Serve with a nice, rustic ficelle or a crusty baguette.

6–8 servings

2–2.5kg fresh clams, cleaned
3–4 tbsp olive oil, plus extra to drizzle
3 banana shallots (or 6 medium shallots),
   peeled and thinly sliced
few thyme sprigs
4 bay leaves
splash of dry white wine
small bunch of flat leaf parsley, leaves only
   chopped

AIOLI:
100ml Mayonnaise (see page 247)
2 garlic cloves, peeled and finely crushed
pinch of paprika
sea salt and freshly ground black pepper

First, make the aïoli. Mix the mayonnaise with the crushed garlic, paprika and salt and pepper to taste until evenly combined. Set aside.

To cook the clams, you will need one very large or two smaller heavy-based saucepans. Heat the olive oil in the pan(s), add the shallots and sauté for 3–4 minutes to soften. Tip in the clams, add the thyme and bay leaves with a splash of wine and cover with a tight-fitting lid. Give the pan a good shake and let the clams steam for 4–5 minutes until the shells have opened. Take the pan off the heat.

Using a slotted spoon, transfer the clams to serving bowls, throwing away any that haven't opened.

Stir enough aïoli into the pan juices to thicken them (about 3–4 tbsp), then add the chopped parsley. Spoon the sauce over the clams and drizzle with a little olive oil to serve. Hand round the rest of the aïoli separately.

TIP To clean the clams, put them in a large bowl of cold water, leave for 5 minutes, then drain. Repeat twice more, replacing with fresh water each time. Discard any open clams.

59

ROAST RUMP OF LAMB WITH HERB COUSCOUS

66 The rump (or chump) of lamb is tender, sweet and juicy – perfect for a quick, succulent roast. Our suppliers generally provide us with lovely 3–4cm thick rumps. Hopefully your butcher will do the same, but the rumps you are likely to find at your local supermarket will probably be thinner steaks. If you buy these, you'll need to reduce the cooking time slightly. **99**

6–8 servings

6–8 rumps of lamb, about 200g each
few rosemary sprigs
4–5 garlic cloves, halved but not peeled
1 tbsp black peppercorns
olive oil, to drizzle
sea salt and freshly ground black pepper

HERB COUSCOUS:
600ml lamb or chicken stock
350g couscous
2–3 tbsp Classic vinaigrette (see page 247)
large handful of parsley, leaves chopped
large handful of mint, leaves chopped
handful of coriander, leaves chopped

TIP If you do not have a large enough ovenproof pan to take all the rumps, transfer them to a roasting pan after browning on the hob.

Lightly score the fat of the lamb in a criss-cross pattern. Place in a large dish and scatter over the rosemary, garlic and peppercorns. Drizzle all over with olive oil and season with pepper. Cover with cling film and leave to marinate in the fridge for at least 2 hours, preferably overnight.

Heat the oven to 200°C/Gas 6. Heat a large ovenproof pan on the hob. Remove the lamb rumps from the marinade, drain and brown them in the hot pan in two or three batches for 2–3 minutes on each side. Return all the lamb to the pan and put into the oven for about 8–10 minutes to finish cooking. The rumps should feel slightly springy when pressed. Cover the lamb loosely with foil and set aside to rest in a warm place for 10–15 minutes before serving.

Prepare the couscous while the lamb is cooking. Bring the stock to the boil. Put the couscous into a large bowl and pour over the boiling stock. Cover the bowl with cling film and leave to soak for 10–15 minutes. Fluff up the couscous grains with a fork, drizzle over the vinaigrette and season with salt and pepper to taste. Reserving a little for garnish, add the chopped herbs and fork through.

Slice the lamb thickly on the diagonal. Pile the herb couscous on to warm plates and arrange the lamb on top. Serve with the aubergine purée if you like, and sprinkle with the remaining herbs.

Spiced aubergine purée

Dice the aubergines, sprinkle lightly with sea salt and put into a colander set over a bowl or the sink. Leave to drain for at least 30 minutes – the aubergines will release their bitter juices. Heat enough olive oil in a heavy-based deep pan for deep-frying (7–10cm depth will be sufficient). Pat the aubergines dry with kitchen paper and deep-fry them, in several batches, until golden brown. Tip into a sieve set over a bowl and leave to drain off the excess oil for several hours, preferably overnight at room temperature.

Soak the sultanas in a little boiling water for about 30 minutes. Heat a little olive oil in a pan, add the onions and season with salt and pepper. Leave to sweat over a medium-low heat, stirring occasionally, until lightly caramelised, about 15–20 minutes. Meanwhile, lightly score the top and bottom of the tomatoes with a cross and immerse in a bowl of boiling water for 30 seconds. Remove with a slotted spoon and refresh under cold running water. Peel off the skins, discard the seeds and finely chop the tomato flesh.

Add the cumin to the caramelised onions and stir over a medium heat for 2–3 minutes. Mix in the aubergines and tomatoes. Drain the sultanas and add them to the pan to heat through. Tip the mixture into a blender or food processor and whiz to a purée. Return to the pan and season with salt and pepper to taste. Reheat the purée and stir through the chopped herbs before serving.

6–8 servings

2 large aubergines, trimmed
sea salt and freshly ground black pepper
olive oil, for deep-frying and cooking
30g sultanas
150g onions, peeled and chopped
3 ripe plum tomatoes
2 tsp ground cumin
handful of coriander, leaves chopped
handful of basil, leaves chopped

TIP If you find the aubergine purée is too wet, stir it over a high heat for a few minutes to cook off the excess moisture.

"Bursting with summer berries, this must be the crowning glory of English puddings. We often make individual puddings using brioche for a posh, restaurant-style dessert, but day-old slices of white bread are perfect for soaking up the juices from the berries. If using fresh bread, you may find it easier to firm up the bread in the refrigerator before slicing."

6–8 servings

1kg mixed berries, such as raspberries, blueberries, redcurrants, blackberries and strawberries
50g caster sugar
4 tbsp crème de cassis (or water)
1 loaf of white bread (about 800g)
pouring cream, to serve

TIP Ripe, juicy berries are essential for this pudding. Halve or quarter any larger fruit, such as strawberries.

Toss all the berries gently in a bowl with the sugar and cassis. Heat a non-stick pan until hot, then add the berries and liquor. Cook over a medium heat for 1½–2 minutes until the fruit softens slightly and starts to bleed. Tip the fruit into a non-reactive sieve set over a non-metallic bowl and allow the juices to drip through for 10 minutes.

Line a pudding basin (1.8 litre capacity or a similar-sized mixing bowl) with cling film. Trim off the crusts from the bread and cut into 1cm thick slices along the length of the loaf (rather than in the usual way). You will need about 5 or 6 long slices. Using an 8cm round pastry cutter, stamp out a circle from one slice to line the base of the pudding basin and another circle to cover the top (with an overlapping join if necessary). Trim the rest of the bread slices so they will fit around the sides, with a slight overlap. (Use any leftover bread to make fresh breadcrumbs.)

Quickly dip one side of the bread slices in the fruit syrup and use to line the bottom and sides of the basin, placing the soaked side of the slices against the basin. Spoon the fruit into the basin, then dip the top bread slices into the juice and use to cover the fruit completely. Spoon the remaining juice over to soak the bread slices. Cover with cling film, place a similar-sized saucer on top and weigh down with a tin. Chill overnight.

When ready to serve, remove the covering cling film, then invert the pudding on to a rimmed plate. Remove the bowl and cling film. Serve at the table, with a jug of pouring cream on the side.

"Who are you doing it with this Sunday?"

07 Classic Sunday lunch

There is nothing quite like a traditional rib of beef for Sunday lunch and with a little organisation, you needn't spend all morning in the kitchen preparing the meal. As it is a substantial affair, you can easily forgo the starter. This menu serves 4–6.

Pigeon salad with hazelnut vinaigrette
Roast beef with Yorkshire pudding & red wine gravy
+ Sautéed cabbage with caramelised onions
+ Glazed carrots with thyme & garlic
+ Roast potatoes with garlic & rosemary

Helen's Eve's pudding

planning your menu

A FEW DAYS AHEAD
• Order the pigeon from your butcher or poulterer and get him to carve out the breasts. Reserve the rib of beef too.

THE DAY BEFORE...
• Make pastry for the pudding and chill.

SEVERAL HOURS IN ADVANCE...
• Shape the pastry case and chill. Make the apple filling.
• Make the dressing for the starter.
• Peel the potatoes and carrots and immerse in cold water.

TWO HOURS AHEAD...
• Bring the beef and pigeon breasts to room temperature.
• Bake the pastry case and cool.
• Make the Yorkshire pudding batter.
• Prepare the salad ingredients for the starter, ready to assemble.

AN HOUR AHEAD...
• Put the beef into the oven to roast.
• Parboil the carrots.
• Blanch and refresh the cabbage and prepare the flavouring ingredients.
• Roast the potatoes.
• Assemble the eve's pudding ready for the meringue topping.

JUST BEFORE SERVING...
• Put the beef to rest and bake the Yorkshire puddings.
• Assemble the salad and pan-fry the pigeon. Plate the starter and serve.
• Take the Yorkshires out of the oven, lower the temperature (for the pudding).
• Finish cooking the vegetables, make the gravy, carve the beef and serve the main course.
• Make the meringue topping for the pudding and bake. Allow to cool for a few minutes, then serve.

PIGEON SALAD WITH HAZELNUT VINAIGRETTE

" Wood pigeons are a real delicacy during the autumn months. We usually carve out the plump breasts and serve them pan-fried on a salad or a bed of lentils. This warm salad also makes a delicious light lunch. "

4–6 servings

breasts from 8–12 large wood pigeons
sea salt and freshly ground black pepper
olive oil, for cooking
knob of butter
2 heads of oak leaf lettuce, washed
  and torn
4 large cooked beetroot, peeled and diced
75g roasted hazelnuts, lightly crushed
few wild rocket leaves (optional)

HAZELNUT VINAIGRETTE:
50ml sherry vinegar
100ml olive oil
50ml hazelnut oil

TIP If possible, get your butcher to carve out the pigeon breasts for you to save time. Ask for the carcasses – they will make a flavourful stock.

For the vinaigrette, whisk the ingredients together and season with salt and pepper to taste. Set aside.

Season the pigeon breasts with salt and pepper. Heat a heavy-based frying pan with a little olive oil until hot. Add the pigeon breasts, skin side down, and fry for about 3 minutes until the skin is crisp. Turn them over and cook the other side for about 2–3 minutes, adding a knob of butter towards the end. As the butter melts, spoon it over the pigeon breasts to baste them. They should feel slightly springy when pressed. Transfer the pigeon breasts to a warm plate and leave to rest, lightly covered with foil, while you assemble the salad.

For the salad, toss the lettuce together with the beetroot, a handful of the crushed hazelnuts and some of the vinaigrette. Divide the salad among individual plates.

Slice the pigeon breasts thickly into 4–5 even pieces. Drizzle a little vinaigrette over them to keep the meat moist. Arrange the pigeon breasts on top of the salad and scatter over the remaining hazelnuts. Drizzle over a little vinaigrette and finish with a few rocket leaves if you like.

ROAST BEEF
WITH YORKSHIRE PUDDING & RED WINE GRAVY

❝ According to photographer Jill's mum, you need 'love and hot fat' to make perfect crisp Yorkshire puddings...I can't argue with that! ❞

4–6 servings

1.2–1.5kg rib of beef, on the bone
sea salt and freshly ground black pepper
2 tbsp olive oil

YORKSHIRE PUDDINGS:
225g plain flour
½ tsp salt
4 eggs, beaten
300ml milk
about 4 tbsp vegetable oil (or beef
   dripping), for cooking

GRAVY:
few thyme sprigs
4 garlic cloves (unpeeled)
2 red onions, peeled and sliced
4 plum tomatoes, halved
½ bottle of red wine (about 350ml)
1.2 litres beef stock

Heat the oven to 200°C/Gas 6. Season the beef with salt and pepper and sear in a hot roasting pan with a little olive oil to brown on all sides, about 3–4 minutes on each side. Transfer to the oven and roast, allowing 15 minutes per 450g for rare or 20 minutes per 450g for medium.

For the Yorkshire batter, sift the flour and salt into a large bowl. Add the eggs and half the milk and beat until smooth. Mix in the remaining milk and leave the batter to rest.

When the beef is cooked, transfer to a warmed plate and leave to rest, lightly covered with foil, in a warm place while you cook the puddings and make the gravy. Increase the oven setting to 230°C/Gas 8. Put 1 tsp oil or, better still, hot fat from the beef roasting pan into each section of a 12-hole Yorkshire pudding tray (or muffin tray) and put into the oven on the top shelf until very hot (almost smoking).

Whisk the batter again in the meantime. As soon as you take the tray from the oven, ladle in the batter to three-quarters fill the tins (it should sizzle) and immediately put back into the oven. Bake for 15–20 minutes until the Yorkshire puddings are well risen, golden brown and crisp. (Don't open the oven door until the end or they might collapse.)

To make the gravy, pour off excess fat from the roasting pan, place on a medium heat and add the thyme, garlic, onions and tomatoes. Cook for 4–5 minutes, then pour in the wine and bring to a simmer. Squash the tomatoes using a potato masher to help thicken the sauce. Pour in the stock and bubble for about 10 minutes until reduced by half. Pass the gravy through a sieve, pressing the vegetables to extract their flavour. Bring back to the boil and reduce to a gravy consistency. Check the seasoning.

Carve the beef thinly. Serve with the gravy, Yorkshire puddings, sautéed cabbage, glazed carrots and roast potatoes.

Sautéed cabbage with caramelised onions

4–6 servings

1 Savoy cabbage, trimmed and shredded
2 red onions, peeled and sliced
olive oil, to drizzle
handful of sage leaves, chopped
knob of butter
sea salt and freshly ground black pepper

Blanch the cabbage in a pan of boiling water for 2 minutes, drain and refresh under running cold water, then drain well. Sweat the sliced onions in a pan with a little olive oil until softened and caramelised. Add the chopped sage and heat for another 2–3 minutes. Melt a knob of butter in a separate pan, add the cooked cabbage and sauté for 3–4 minutes. Add the onion mixture and season with salt and pepper to taste. Sauté for another couple of minutes until the cabbage is tender and warmed through, then serve.

Glazed carrots with thyme & garlic

Put the carrots into a large pan and pour over enough stock to cover. Add the thyme, garlic and bay leaf and parboil for about 8 minutes (until the carrots are two-thirds cooked). Leave the carrots to cool in the stock, then drain thoroughly and pat dry. Heat a little olive oil in a sauté pan, add the carrots and season well. Sauté for a couple of minutes, then add some butter and a sprinkling of sugar (for a caramelised finish). Baste the carrots with the melted butter and cook for a further 3–4 minutes until they are tender and beautifully glazed.

4–6 servings

600g (about 18–20) small carrots, peeled
1–1.5 litres vegetable stock
1 thyme sprig
½ head of garlic (cut horizontally)
1 bay leaf
olive oil, for cooking
sea salt and freshly ground black pepper
few knobs of butter
1–2 tsp caster sugar (optional)

Roast potatoes with garlic & rosemary

4–6 servings

2–3 tbsp vegetable oil or beef dripping
1.5kg potatoes, such as Charlotte or Desirée, peeled
1 garlic clove, peeled and crushed
few rosemary sprigs
sea salt and freshly ground black pepper

Heat the oven to 200°C/Gas 6. Put the oil in a sturdy baking tray on the hob over a medium heat. When hot, add the potatoes and turn to coat well. Add the garlic and rosemary to the tray and season the potatoes well. Put the tray into the oven and roast, turning the potatoes occasionally, for 40–45 minutes until they are golden, crisp and cooked through. Drain on kitchen paper and serve.

HELEN'S EVE'S PUDDING

66 My mother's apple pudding is very different from mine and as far as she's concerned hers is definitely better! It has a sweet pastry crust filled with stewed apples and topped with meringue, resembling a lemon meringue pie. It is best eaten soon after baking. **99**

SWEET PASTRY:
150g butter, softened to room temperature
100g caster sugar
4 egg yolks, beaten
300g plain flour, plus extra to dust
pinch of salt

FILLING:
4 Granny Smith apples
2 tbsp caster sugar

MERINGUE TOPPING:
2 egg whites
4 tbsp caster sugar
few drops of vanilla extract

To make the pastry, cream together the butter and sugar, using a hand-held electric mixer until pale and creamy. Gradually add the egg yolks, then incorporate the flour and salt until the mixture is evenly blended and crumbly, adding 1–2 tbsp cold water if it seems too dry. Bring the dough together with your hand, press into a ball, flatten slightly and wrap in cling film. Chill for at least 30 minutes.

Roll out the pastry thinly on a lightly floured surface and use to line a 20cm tart tin with removable base. Line the pastry with baking parchment or foil and fill with baking beans. Refrigerate for at least 20 minutes.

Make the filling in the meantime. Peel, core and chop the apples and place in a pan with the sugar and 1 tbsp water. Cook gently for about 10 minutes until the apples are soft but still holding their shape. Tip on to a plate and leave to cool completely.

Heat the oven to 180°C/Gas 4. Bake the pastry case blind for 15 minutes until golden at the edges, then remove the foil and beans and bake for another 5 minutes or until the base is cooked. Set aside to cool. Increase the oven setting to 200°C/Gas 6.

For the meringue, beat the egg whites, using a hand-held electric whisk until stiff. Gradually beat in the sugar, a spoonful at a time, with the vanilla until fully incorporated and the meringue is stiff.

Spread the apple filling in the pastry case and top with the meringue. Peak the meringue with a fork to give it an attractive finish. Bake for 15–20 minutes until the meringue is golden brown. Cool slightly, then slice into individual portions and serve warm.

5 ways with...POTATOES

Red onion & sweet potato rösti
Serves 4–6

Heat a little olive oil in a wide heavy-based frying pan and sauté 2 finely sliced red onions and 1 finely chopped garlic clove for 5 minutes or until softened. Tip into a bowl and allow to cool. Peel and grate 750g sweet potatoes, wrap in a clean cloth and squeeze out excess liquid. Mix with the sautéed onions, 1 medium beaten egg, 15g melted butter and seasoning.

Heat a little olive oil and a knob of butter in a wide heavy-based frying pan. Using one or more 10cm greased plain metal cutters, shape the sweet potato mixture into neat cakes in the pan, pressing the mixture down in the rings. Cook over a medium-low heat for about 5–6 minutes until the underside is golden brown, then remove the rings and flip the rösti with a palette knife. Cook the other side for 2–3 minutes until crisp. Drain the rösti on kitchen paper and keep warm while cooking the remaining mixture. Equally good with meat, chicken and vegetables dishes.

Duchess potatoes
Serves 4–6

Heat the oven to 220°C/Gas 7. Peel 1.5kg floury potatoes (such as King Edward) and halve or quarter if large. Boil in salted water for 12–15 minutes until tender. Drain, then return to the pan and place over a low heat for a minute or so to drive off excess moisture. Mash the potatoes well, using a potato ricer if possible. For a smoother finish, push the mash through a fine sieve.

Return the mashed potatoes to the pan and place over a medium heat. Stir in 150g butter and season with salt, pepper and a little grated nutmeg if you like. Take the pan off the heat and mix in 2 beaten medium eggs. Spoon the enriched mash into a large piping bag fitted with a 2cm fluted nozzle and, while still warm, pipe into whirls on a greased baking sheet. Bake for 5–7 minutes until golden and crisp at the edges. An elegant accompaniment to meat, poultry, game or fish.

Roast Charlotte potatoes with chorizo
Serves 4-6

Heat the oven to 200°C/Gas 6. Boil 1kg medium Charlotte potatoes in salted water for 7–9 minutes. Drain and peel when cool enough to handle, then cut in half. Chop 200g fresh (or smoked) chorizo sausage into bite-sized pieces. Heat a thin layer of olive oil in an ovenproof frying pan, add the chorizo and fry until it starts to release oil. Toss in the potatoes, season well, then roast in the oven for 15–20 minutes until golden brown. Sprinkle with chopped parsley. Delicious with Mediterranean-style chicken and fish.

Sautéed potatoes with paprika
Serves 4-6

Scrub 1kg Charlotte (or other waxy) potatoes and boil in salted water for 7–9 minutes. Drain and peel while still hot (wearing rubber gloves). Cut the potatoes into 1cm cubes and drizzle with a little olive oil. Spread out on a tray, season well and leave to cool. Heat a little olive oil in a wide frying pan over a medium-high heat. Add the diced potatoes and cook, turning occasionally, until golden brown, crisp at the edges and tender. Drain on kitchen paper. Serve warm, sprinkled with mild paprika and sea salt. Lovely with fish or poultry dishes.

Champ with spring onions & broad beans
Serves 4-6

Peel 1.5kg floury potatoes (such as King Edward) and halve or quarter if large. Boil in salted water for 12–15 minutes until tender; drain thoroughly. Mash the potatoes while still hot, then stir through 50g butter. Bring 450ml milk and 150ml double cream to the boil in another pan. Add 5–6 finely chopped spring onions and 400g skinned broad beans (or peas) and cook for 2 minutes until the beans are tender. With a slotted spoon, transfer the onions and beans to the potatoes, then gradually stir in enough of the creamy milk to achieve a good texture. Season well. Reheat the champ, stir through a handful of chopped chives and top with a large knob of butter to serve. Perfect with rustic stews, braised meat dishes or as part of a hearty brunch.

08 Keep it simple

Fine fish is a smart choice for an impressive quick main course. Follow with a heavenly pudding and everyone will be more than satisfied. Make the starter ahead or for an easy last-minute option, serve Asparagus with herb butter (see page 43). This menu serves 6.

Piquant mushroom & vegetable salad
Black bream with basil & peas 'bonne femme'
Cherry clafoutis

planning your menu

A FEW DAYS AHEAD...
• Order the fish from the fishmonger (get him to fillet it for you). Arrange to collect it on the day if possible, or the day before.

THE DAY BEFORE...
• Prepare the marinated mushrooms for the starter and refrigerate overnight.
• Make the clafoutis batter, stone the cherries and chill.

AN HOUR IN ADVANCE...
• For the peas 'bonne femme', peel the onions and pod fresh peas if using.
• Bring the clafoutis batter to room temperature and divide the cherries among baking dishes, ready to cook.
• For the starter, blanch the vegetables for the starter and toss in the vinaigrette.
• Prepare the fish fillets and wrap in cling film, ready to cook.

HALF AN HOUR AHEAD...
• Take the mushrooms out of the fridge.
• For the peas, cook the lardons and onions; set aside.
• Pour the batter over the cherries and bake the clafoutis.

JUST BEFORE SERVING...
• Assemble the starter.
• Poach the bream fillets while you eat your starter, timing carefully.
• Finish the peas 'bonne femme' and assemble the main course.
• Leave the clafoutis at room temperature while you eat the main course.
• Dust the cherry clafoutis with icing sugar and serve.

PIQUANT MUSHROOM & VEGETABLE SALAD

" I first came across this salad at a restaurant in Paris and I was intrigued by the flavourings used for the mushrooms, all coming together in a sweet-and-sour medley of summer vegetables. The whole coriander seeds provide an invigorating twist to the salad but you can just use ground coriander if you find the seeds too harsh. "

6 servings

MARINATED MUSHROOMS:

30g raisins

30g golden sultanas

600g button mushrooms, cleaned

4 tbsp olive oil

1 large onion, peeled and chopped

1 tsp whole coriander seeds

2 tsp ground coriander

sea salt and freshly ground black pepper

300ml dry white wine

1 bouquet garni (parsley stalks, celery, thyme sprigs and a bay leaf)

juice of ½ lemon, or to taste

4 large ripe tomatoes, about 500g in total

1 tbsp tomato purée

pinch of caster sugar, or to taste

SALAD:

½ head of cauliflower, cut into florets

200g baby leeks, white part only, trimmed

150g pearl onions, peeled

250g small asparagus tips

200g fresh or frozen peas (thawed if frozen)

4 tbsp Classic vinaigrette (see page 247)

handful of mint leaves, shredded

Put the dried fruit in a small bowl, add boiling water to cover and leave to soak for at least 20 minutes, then drain. Twist the stems off the mushrooms and cut any larger ones in half.

Heat the olive oil in a large pan. Add the onion with the coriander seeds, ground coriander and some seasoning and cook gently for 5 minutes or until starting to soften. Add the white wine and bouquet garni. Boil for 7–10 minutes until reduced by half, then lower the heat. Add the mushrooms and lemon juice, cover and sweat for 5 minutes.

Score the tomatoes, top and bottom, with a cross and immerse in a bowl of boiling water for 40 seconds. Remove, refresh under cold water, then peel off the skins. Halve and deseed, then put into a food processor with the tomato purée and whiz until smooth.

Transfer the mushrooms to a sieve set over a bowl to drain, using a slotted spoon. Tip the puréed tomatoes into the mushroom liquor and boil over a high heat for 7–10 minutes until thickened, stirring frequently. Discard the bouquet garni. Return the mushrooms to the pan and add the raisins and sultanas. Reheat for a few minutes. Check the seasoning and balance the acidity with a pinch of sugar or a little more lemon juice. Transfer to a bowl to cool, then cover and refrigerate overnight to allow the flavours to mingle.

Take the mushrooms out of the fridge half an hour before serving. For the salad, blanch the vegetables separately in boiling salted water for about 2–3 minutes. Drain, refresh in iced water and drain well, then tip into a large bowl and dress with the vinaigrette. Add the mushrooms and tomato marinade and toss to combine. Serve with a generous sprinkling of shredded mint.

BLACK BREAM
WITH BASIL & PEAS 'BONNE FEMME'

 " Black bream has a delicate, slightly sweet flavour that really comes through when the fish is gently poached or steamed. French-style peas with snippets of bacon and little onions are the perfect base for the fish. "

6 servings

6 black bream fillets, skin on, about 175g each
sea salt and freshly ground black pepper
small handful of basil leaves
olive oil, to drizzle

PEAS 'BONNE FEMME':
olive oil, for cooking
250g unsmoked bacon lardons
150g pearl onions, peeled
few thyme sprigs, leaves only
600g fresh or frozen peas (thawed, if frozen)

TIP At our restaurants, we wrap the fish and herbs in cling film before poaching, to seal in the juices and prevent the fish from becoming waterlogged. if you're not comfortable with the idea of cooking in cling film, steaming would achieve a comparable result.

Check the fish for small bones, removing any that you find with tweezers. Score the skin at 1cm intervals. Season with salt and pepper and place a few basil leaves on the flesh side. Place each bream fillet on a large piece of cling film and drizzle with olive oil. Wrap up to enclose the fillets in the cling film, twisting the ends tightly to seal.

For the peas, heat a little olive oil in a frying pan and fry the lardons for 8–10 minutes until golden brown and crisp. Remove and drain on kitchen paper. Add the onions and thyme to the pan and cook on a medium heat, stirring occasionally, for 10 minutes until the onions are tender.

In the meantime, bring a large pan of water to the boil, then reduce the heat to a low simmer. Add the wrapped bream fillets and gently poach for about 10 minutes until the fish is opaque and cooked through. If the centre is not cooked through, poach for a further 2–3 minutes.

Add the peas and bacon to the onions and cook for 2–3 minutes until the peas are tender. Season well.

Divide the peas 'bonne femme' among six warm plates. Unwrap the bream fillets and place on top of the vegetables, skin side up. Drizzle with a little olive oil and sprinkle with sea salt. Serve immediately.

CHERRY CLAFOUTIS

" To the French, cherry clafoutis is what bread and butter pudding is to the British – a real comfort pudding that has stood the test of time. When fresh cherries are out of season, we often use bottled cherries marinated in kirsch to make clafoutis. "

6 servings

50g ground almonds
15g plain flour
generous pinch of fine sea salt
100g caster sugar
2 large eggs
3 large egg yolks
250ml double cream
unsalted butter, to grease
icing sugar, to dust
300g fresh cherries, washed and pitted

TIP The clafoutis batter can be made in a food processor. Pulse the dry ingredients for a few seconds to combine, then add the eggs and cream and whiz until smooth.

Put the ground almonds, flour, salt and sugar into a large bowl and mix well to combine. Make an indentation in the centre. In another bowl, beat the eggs, egg yolks and cream together, then pour into the hollow in the dry mixture. Whisk until the batter is smooth. If preparing in advance, transfer the batter to a jug (or cover the bowl with cling film) and chill overnight.

Heat the oven to 190°C/Gas 5. Generously butter 4–6 shallow ovenproof dishes and dust the base and sides with icing sugar. Divide the stoned cherries among the prepared dishes. Give the batter a stir, then pour over the cherries. Place the dishes on a large baking sheet and bake in the oven for 20–30 minutes until golden brown and risen. Check that the clafoutis have set in the middle, if not bake for another 5 minutes.

Leave the clafoutis to stand for 5–10 minutes. Add a dusting of icing sugar before serving.

NEARLY 10% OF PEOPLE USE FROZEN OR PRE-PREPARED FOOD EVERY DAY OF THE WEEK.

"Using fresh ingredients is the only way to guarantee a great taste. I can't understand how on earth people can ignore fresh food. That's where all the flavour is, all the goodness and it's a crime not to use it. Fresh food is what your family should be eating and if it means shopping more frequently or travelling to a couple of markets, then trust me, it's worth it."

09 Easy barbecue

Perfect for a summer barbecue, this food is equally good cooked indoors on a griddle or under the grill, so you're not dependant on the weather. For a more substantial meal, add butcher's sausages and Griddled chicken (see page 162). This menu serves 6–8.

Crushed peas & mozzarella on toast with pecorino

Honey mustard pork chops

Ginger & port marinated lamb skewers

+ New potato salad

+ Green bean, spinach & red onion salad

Blueberry & redcurrant Eton mess

planning your menu

THE DAY BEFORE...
• Marinate the meats in the fridge overnight.
• Make the meringues for the dessert (unless using ready-made).

SEVERAL HOURS IN ADVANCE...
• For the starter, prepare the crushed peas, cover and set aside.
• Make the dressing for the potato salad and wash the potatoes ready for cooking.

TWO HOURS AHEAD...
• Blanch the beans and prepare the other salad ingredients, ready to assemble.
• Make the berry purée for the dessert.

ABOUT HALF AN HOUR AHEAD...
• Whip the cream and crush the meringues, so the dessert is all ready to assemble.
• Drain the lamb and thread on to kebab skewers. Prepare chops for cooking.
• Cook the potatoes and toss with the dressing while hot.
• Prepare the green bean salad.

JUST BEFORE SERVING...
• Assemble the starter and serve your guests, while you start cooking the meat on the barbecue or griddle.
• Serve the barbecued meats with the salads.
• Assemble the pudding and serve.

CRUSHED PEAS & MOZZARELLA ON TOAST WITH PECORINO

"These little bites are a take on bruschetta, with a summery aspect from the green peas. You could take the dish a step further by blending the peas with the leaves from a bunch of mint or flat leaf parsley, which will turn the crushed peas a deeper shade of green."

6–8 servings

400g shelled fresh peas
sea salt and freshly ground black pepper
125g mascarpone
4 tbsp olive oil, plus extra to drizzle
12–16 thick slices of ciabatta
100g bocconcini (baby mozzarella)
4 tbsp freshly grated pecorino

Cook the peas in boiling salted water for 3–5 minutes until they are really tender, then drain and tip into a food processor. Add the mascarpone, olive oil and seasoning and whiz to a rough paste. Transfer to a bowl and set aside.

Preheat a griddle or grill until hot. Toast the ciabatta slices for about 2 minutes on each side, then drizzle with a little olive oil.

Spread the crushed peas on the toasted ciabatta slices. Roughly tear the mozzarella balls in half and place on top. Sprinkle with the pecorino and drizzle with a little more olive oil. Grind over a little more seasoning and serve immediately.

TIP You'll need approximately 1kg peas in the pod to give this shelled weight.

HONEY MUSTARD PORK CHOPS

"These tasty chops – and the lamb skewers below – are two of my favourite things to cook on a barbecue or griddle. The marinades not only tenderise the meat, they also impart great flavours."

6–8 servings

6–8 pork chops, about 200g each
olive oil, to brush

MARINADE:
2 tbsp Dijon mustard
4 tbsp wholegrain mustard
6 tbsp runny honey
4 tbsp Worcestershire sauce
4 tbsp light soy sauce

Mix the marinade
ingredients together in shallow bowl. Add the pork chops and turn to coat well. Cover with cling film and marinate in the fridge for a few hours or overnight.

Heat a griddle pan
or barbecue (or grill) until hot. Scrape the excess marinade off the pork chops and save it. Brush the chops with a little olive oil. Cook on the barbecue or griddle (or grill) for 4–5 minutes on each side or until cooked through, basting with the marinade occasionally. Rest the chops in a warm spot for 5–10 minutes (while you cook the lamb).

Serve the pork chops
with the lamb skewers or other barbecued meats, accompanied by side salads and crusty bread.

GINGER & PORT MARINATED LAMB SKEWERS

6–8 servings

8–10 wooden kebab skewers
800g boneless tender lamb
olive oil, to brush

MARINADE:
200ml port
2 tbsp grated fresh root ginger
4 garlic cloves, peeled and crushed
few rosemary sprigs, bruised with
   the back of a knife
sea salt and freshly ground black pepper
2 tbsp olive oil

Soak the kebab skewers
in cold water. Combine the port, ginger, garlic and rosemary in a wide shallow bowl. Cut the lamb into 2cm cubes, add to the bowl and turn to coat in the marinade. Cover with cling film and leave to marinate in the fridge for 3–4 hours or overnight (no longer, otherwise the port will overpower the flavour of the lamb).

Drain the lamb
and pat dry with kitchen paper. Season the meat and brush with a little olive oil, then thread on to the skewers. Cook on a preheated barbecue or griddle (or grill) for about 2–3 minutes on each side. The lamb should be slightly springy when pressed.

New potato salad

Cook the potatoes in boiling salted
water for 8–10 minutes or until just tender. In the meantime, whisk the dressing ingredients together, seasoning with salt and pepper to taste. When cooked, drain the potatoes and place in a mixing bowl with the shallot and chopped mint. While the potatoes are still hot, add the dressing and toss to mix. Serve warm or at room temperature.

6–8 servings

**1kg baby new potatoes, such as Jersey Royals or
  Charlotte, washed**
sea salt and freshly ground black pepper
1 large shallot, peeled and finely chopped
handful of mint or tarragon, leaves chopped

DRESSING:
1 tbsp tarragon vinegar or cider vinegar
2 tsp Dijon mustard
1 tsp wholegrain mustard
2 tbsp olive oil
2 tbsp walnut oil
2 tsp runny honey

Green bean, spinach & red onion salad

6–8 servings

300g green beans, topped
sea salt and freshly ground black pepper
3 red onions, peeled and very thinly sliced
**500g baby spinach leaves, washed and
  spun dry**

DRESSING:
3 tbsp balsamic vinegar
100ml olive oil

Blanch the beans in a pan of boiling salted water
for 2 minutes. Drain and refresh under cold running water. Drain the beans well and tip them into a large bowl. Add the sliced red onions and spinach leaves and toss to mix. Whisk the balsamic vinegar and olive oil together with some seasoning to make the dressing. Pour this over the salad and toss well just before serving.

BLUEBERRY & REDCURRANT ETON MESS

" A scrumptious muddle of berries and cream originating from the boarding school of the same name. I often make it for my children, using berries we've picked ourselves. Add the crushed meringues just before serving, to keep them light and crisp. "

6–8 servings

300g redcurrants, plus sprigs to finish
300g blueberries
2 tbsp caster sugar, plus extra to coat
4 tbsp kirsch (optional)
600ml double cream
2 tbsp icing sugar
2 meringue nests (ideally homemade, see page 248)

Put half the fruit into a dry non-stick pan with the sugar and kirsch if using. Cook over a high heat for 1½–2 minutes until the berries soften and begin to bleed. Crush lightly with a fork and push the fruit through a non-reactive sieve into a large bowl. Leave to cool completely.

Whip the cream together with the icing sugar in another bowl until it forms soft peaks. Crush the meringue nests and fold them through the cream with the remaining berries. Fold or ripple through the cooled berry coulis.

Spoon the mixture into a large glass bowl or on to individual serving plates. Coat the remaining redcurrants with a little caster sugar and use to decorate each plate.

10 Seafood special

Monkfish is teamed with mussels for a stylish seafood meal. A creamy risotto makes a lovely autumnal starter, or you might prefer to extend the seafood theme and start with Roasted tomato salad with prawns and anchovies (see page 229). For a lighter dessert, I recommend my Lemon tart (see page 137). This menu serves 4–6.

Pumpkin risotto with Parmesan
Monkfish with curried mussels
Ginger chocolate cheesecake

planning your menu

A FEW DAYS AHEAD
• Order the monkfish from your fishmonger and get him to fillet it for you. Arrange to pick it up on the day if possible, or the day before.

THE DAY BEFORE...
• Make the cheesecake and the flavoured crème fraîche and chill.

SEVERAL HOURS IN ADVANCE...
• Make the pumpkin purée for the risotto.

TWO HOURS AHEAD...
• Clean the mussels.

AN HOUR AHEAD...
• Trim the monkfish and set aside at room temperature.
• Prepare and chop the vegetables for the main course.
• Cook and shell the mussels.

30 MINUTES AHEAD...
• Sauté the main course vegetables and reduce the liquor. Dust the monkfish with the curry/salt mix, ready to cook.
• Cook the risotto.

JUST BEFORE SERVING...
• Plate the risotto and serve.
• Pan-fry the monkfish, wilt the spinach, finish the main course and serve.
• Unmould the cheesecake, slice and serve with the ginger crème fraîche.

PUMPKIN RISOTTO WITH PARMESAN

" I love making this risotto towards the end of autumn when pumpkins are ripe and flavourful. We usually cook with iron bark pumpkins at the restaurant – jack o'lantern Halloween pumpkins are too watery and stringy. You can use butternut squash, allowing a little longer for it to cook. "

4–6 servings

large wedge of ripe pumpkin, about
  500–600g
olive oil, for cooking and to drizzle
1.3 litres Chicken (or vegetable) stock
  (see page 246)
300g risotto rice (Arborio or Carnaroli)
sea salt and freshly ground black pepper
few knobs of butter
50g Parmesan, freshly grated, plus
  shavings to serve
small handful of sage leaves

TIP Cooked pumpkin purée freezes well, so if you find yourself having to buy a whole pumpkin that's more than you need, cook and purée the lot, freezing the rest for later use.

Cut the pumpkin

into 1cm cubes. Heat a little olive oil in a large pan over a medium heat. Add the pumpkin and cook gently for 5–7 minutes until just softened, stirring occasionally. Set aside one-third. Put the rest of the pumpkin into a blender and whiz until smooth, adding a touch of hot water as necessary (to get the purée moving in the blender).

Bring the stock

to a simmer in a pan and keep it at a gentle simmer over a low heat. Heat a little olive oil in a larger saucepan and tip in the rice. Cook, stirring frequently, for a minute, then add a ladleful of hot stock and stir until it is almost all absorbed before adding another ladleful. Repeat until you've reached your last few ladlefuls of stock. Taste the rice to see if it is *al dente*. If not, add more stock. Add the pumpkin purée and reserved pumpkin, stirring through and seasoning to taste. Stir in a few knobs of butter and the grated Parmesan. Keep warm.

Heat a thin layer of olive oil

in a small frying pan until hot. Fry the sage leaves for a few seconds until crisp then drain on kitchen paper.

Ladle the risotto

on to warm plates and tap the bottom of each plate gently to spread it out. Drizzle with a little olive oil and scatter over the Parmesan and sage leaves, then serve.

MONKFISH WITH CURRIED MUSSELS

66 I love this combination. A light coating of curry spice gives the monkfish a golden crust and imparts a subtle taste that doesn't overpower the delicate flavour of the fish. There's plenty going on here, so you don't really need any accompaniments, though you could serve Pommes purée (see page 43) on the side if you like. *99*

4–6 servings

4–6 monkfish tail fillets, about 150g each
500g mussels, cleaned with beards
  removed
few thyme sprigs
2 bay leaves
75ml dry white wine
1 large carrot, peeled and chopped
1 leek, trimmed and chopped
½ celeriac, peeled and chopped
3 tbsp olive oil
5 tsp curry powder
2 pinches of saffron strands
sea salt and freshly ground black pepper
400g baby spinach, washed
knob of butter
200ml double cream
handful of chives, chopped

Trim the monkfish fillets if necessary,
removing any grey membrane. Heat the oven to 180°C/Gas 4.

Heat a large saucepan until hot, then
add the mussels, a couple of thyme sprigs, the bay leaves and white wine. Cover the pan with a tight-fitting lid and give it a good shake. Cook for about 3–4 minutes, shaking once or twice, until the mussels have opened. Strain and reserve the juices. Remove the mussels from their shells and set aside; discard any unopened ones.

Sauté the vegetables in 1 tbsp olive oil
until soft. Sprinkle with 1 tsp curry powder and the saffron. Add a thyme sprig, tip in the mussel juice and simmer until reduced by half.

Meanwhile, mix the remaining 4 tsp curry powder
with 1 tsp salt. Pat the monkfish tails dry with kitchen paper and dust with the curry/salt mix. Heat 2 tbsp olive oil in an ovenproof frying pan and fry the monkfish fillets for 2–3 minutes until golden brown. Transfer the pan to the oven for 4–5 minutes to finish off the cooking. The fish is ready when it feels just firm.

Wilt the spinach gently in a warm pan with a
knob of butter for about 1–2 minutes while the fish is in the oven. At the same time, pour the cream into the sautéed vegetables and bring to a gentle simmer. Add the mussels to warm through, then finally mix in the chives and season to taste.

Divide the spinach among warm plates
and spoon over the creamy mussel mixture. Thickly slice the monkfish and arrange on top. Serve at once.

GINGER CHOCOLATE CHEESECAKE

> " This cheesecake, made by fireman Paul Beer on the first F word series, proved to be more popular than mine! I have to confess it has just the right balance of sweetness and bitterness from the dark chocolate, with a subtle hint of ginger. Baked cheesecakes characteristically sink when they cool so don't be alarmed to see cracks on the surface of your cheesecake. "

6–8 servings

150g stem ginger biscuits, broken up
50g unsalted butter, melted, plus extra
  to grease
250g mascarpone
200g fromage frais
2 large eggs
35g caster sugar
150g dark chocolate with stem ginger,
  broken into pieces

TO SERVE:
200g crème fraîche
1 tbsp stem ginger syrup
5 pieces crystallised stem ginger
  (or 2 pieces stem ginger from the jar)
icing sugar, to dust

Heat the oven to 190°C/Gas 5. Put the biscuits into a food processor and blitz to fine crumbs. Tip into a bowl and mix with the melted butter. Pour the mixture into a lightly greased 20cm round cake tin with a removable base and level out with the back of a spatula or a large spoon. Bake for 5 minutes, then set aside to cool. Lower the oven setting to 170°C/Gas 3.

Whisk the mascarpone and fromage frais together in a bowl until smooth. Add the eggs and sugar and mix well. Melt the chocolate in a bain-marie (or bowl set over a pan of barely simmering water) and then gently fold into the mascarpone mixture.

Pour the filling over the biscuit base and bake for 50–60 minutes. The cheesecake is ready when the filling is just set – it should still have a slight wobble in the centre. Remove from the oven and run a thin knife around the edge of the tin. Leave the cheesecake to cool in the tin, during which time the filling will continue to set.

Before serving, flavour the crème fraîche with the ginger syrup, folding it in until evenly blended. Finely slice the ginger into matchsticks. Carefully unmould the cheesecake on to a plate. Serve cut into slices with the ginger crème fraîche, a scattering of ginger and a dusting of icing sugar.

11 Roast lamb

This enticing menu captures some wonderful flavours of spring – red mullet, new season's lamb and tender rhubarb. If you would rather serve a prepare-ahead starter, Horseradish marinated salmon (see page 181) is a good option. This menu serves 6.

Red mullet with sautéed potatoes & anchovy dressing
Saddle of lamb with apricot & cumin stuffing
+ Spinach with garlic, chilli & pine nuts
+ Balsamic roasted red onions
+ Pommes purée (see page 43)

Rhubarb crème brûlée

planning your menu

A FEW DAYS AHEAD...
• Order the saddle of lamb from your butcher and the fish from the fishmonger (arranging to collect a day ahead, or pick the mullet up fresh on the day if you can).

THE DAY BEFORE...
• Make the stuffing and prepare the lamb so it's stuffed, rolled, tied and all ready to roast. Wrap in cling film and refrigerate.
• Make the crème brûlées and chill, ready to apply the topping the next day.

SEVERAL HOURS IN ADVANCE...
• Check the fish fillets for pin bones; keep in the fridge. Prepare the dressing, saving the tarragon to add at the last minute.
• Prepare and cook the balsamic onions, ready to reheat before serving (unless you have a second oven to cook them in at the same time as the meat).
• Peel the potatoes for the pommes purée and immerse in cold water.

TWO HOURS AHEAD...
• Bring the meat to room temperature.
• Wash the spinach and prepare the flavouring ingredients ready to cook.
• For the starter, parboil the potatoes, peel (but don't slice) and toss in olive oil.

FROM AN HOUR AHEAD...
• Take the red mullet from the fridge and score it. Slice the parboiled potatoes and finish the dressing.
• Sear the lamb and put it into the oven to roast. Prepare and cook the pommes purée; keep warm.

JUST BEFORE SERVING...
• Sauté the potatoes, pan-fry the fish and assemble the starter.
• Rest the meat and reheat the onions while you eat the starter.
• Sauté the spinach, carve the lamb and serve the main course.
• Finish the crème brûlées and serve.

RED MULLET
WITH SAUTEED POTATOES & ANCHOVY DRESSING

“ Really fresh fish needs nothing more than quick, simple cooking. My favourite way of cooking fish fillets is pan-frying, which leaves the fish with a beautifully crisp skin and succulent flesh. Here, pan-fried red mullet is served with sautéed potatoes and an uplifting anchovy dressing, guaranteed to wake up the tastebuds. ”

6 servings

750g even-sized Charlotte potatoes,
   washed
sea salt and freshly ground black pepper
olive oil, for cooking
10 red mullet fillets, about 100g each,
   skin on
large handful of frisée leaves

ANCHOVY DRESSING:
50g can anchovy fillets, drained
1 garlic clove, peeled and crushed
1 tbsp white wine vinegar
100ml olive oil
1 tsp chopped tarragon

Boil the potatoes in a pan of salted water for 7 minutes, drain and briefly refresh under cold running water. While still warm, peel off the skins and cut the potatoes into thick 2cm slices.

Heat a sauté pan with a thin film of olive oil. Add the potato slices, season well with salt and pepper and fry over a medium heat for about 5 minutes on each side until golden brown and cooked through.

For the anchovy dressing, put the anchovies, garlic and wine vinegar into a food processor and whiz to a rough purée. With the motor running, slowly trickle in the olive oil until amalgamated. Transfer the dressing to a bowl and stir in the tarragon.

Check the fish fillets for small pin bones, removing any you find with tweezers. Score the skin at 1cm intervals. Heat a wide frying pan until hot and add a little olive oil. Season the fish fillets and place them in the hot pan, skin side down. Cook for 2–3 minutes until the skin is crisp and the fish is cooked two-thirds of the way through, then turn over and cook the other side for 30 seconds. Lift the fish on to a warm plate.

Arrange the sautéed potatoes in the centre of six warm serving plates. Place two fish fillets on top of each portion and scatter the frisée leaves around the plate. Spoon over the anchovy dressing and serve immediately.

SADDLE OF LAMB WITH APRICOT & CUMIN STUFFING

" A saddle of lamb comes with two loins, from both sides of the backbone, and once the bone is removed, there is a natural cavity that is perfect for stuffing and rolling. Get your butcher to skin and bone the saddle for you and ask for the bones to make stock. The roasted cumin, apricot and pine nut stuffing is superb with the sweet, tender lamb. "

6 servings

1.3 kg saddle of lamb, skinned and boned
2 tbsp cumin seeds
sea salt and freshly ground black pepper
20–22 slices of Parma ham, about 200g
    in total
sea salt and freshly ground black pepper
olive oil, for cooking

STUFFING:
150g apricots, soaked overnight in warm
    water, drained
30g pine nuts, toasted
25g fresh breadcrumbs
1 tbsp olive oil

TIP Any extra stuffing can be formed into balls, rolled in breadcrumbs and roasted alongside the lamb for the last 20 minutes or so.

Trim off the excess fillets at both ends of the saddle so that you can roll the lamb into a neat log. (Use them for another dish.) Toast the cumin seeds in a hot dry pan, tossing occasionally, until fragrant. Using a pestle and mortar, coarsely grind the seeds with a pinch each of sea salt and pepper, then rub half over the lamb.

For the stuffing, finely chop the apricots and pine nuts (or pulse in a food processor to a rough paste), then tip into a bowl. Stir in the breadcrumbs, olive oil, some salt and pepper and the rest of the cumin.

On a large sheet of cling film, arrange all but two of the Parma ham slices in a rectangle, overlapping them slightly. (This needs to be large enough to wrap around the lamb.) Lay the lamb, opened out like a butterfly, on top of the Parma ham. Season the lamb and pile the stuffing in a neat row along the centre. (You may not need all of it.) Fold the sides of the lamb over the stuffing. Wrap the lamb parcel in the Parma ham and outer cling film to form a tight log. Chill for an hour to slightly 'set' the shape.

Heat the oven to 180°C/Gas 4. Remove the cling film from the lamb. Use the remaining slices of Parma ham to cover the two ends and secure the stuffing. Tie the log with kitchen string at 2–3cm intervals – just firmly enough to hold it together during roasting.

Heat a little olive oil in a wide ovenproof frying pan until hot. Sear the lamb for 3–4 minutes on each side until browned, then position seam side down in the centre of the pan and transfer to the oven. Roast for 35–40 minutes, turning and basting the lamb halfway through cooking. It should feel slightly springy when pressed and the meat should be pink in the centre. Rest in a warm place for 10–15 minutes, then slice thickly and serve with the pan juices and accompaniments.

Spinach with garlic, chilli & pine nuts

Sauté the garlic in a little olive oil in a wide pan for a minute until golden brown, then add the chilli and pine nuts. Toss over a medium heat until the nuts are nicely toasted and golden brown. Add the spinach leaves in large handfuls, stirring and wilting each handful before adding the next one. Season well and serve at once.

6 servings

3 garlic cloves, peeled and finely sliced
olive oil, for cooking
½ red chilli, deseeded and finely chopped
50g pine nuts
750g baby spinach, washed
sea salt and freshly ground black pepper

Balsamic roasted red onions

6 servings

6–8 medium red onions
20g unsalted butter
1 tbsp olive oil
few rosemary sprigs
sea salt and freshly ground black pepper
5 tbsp balsamic vinegar

Heat the oven to 140°C/Gas 1. Peel the onions and slice off one-third of the tops to expose the layers. Heat the butter and olive oil in a heavy-based ovenproof pan. Add the onions, cut side down, and sauté for 4–5 minutes until golden brown. Add the rosemary and season the onions with salt and pepper. Deglaze the pan with the balsamic vinegar, cover with foil and transfer to the oven.

Slowly roast the onions for 30 minutes, then remove the foil and turn the onions cut side up. Return the pan to the oven for 1–1¼ hours until the onions are tender. Check halfway through as you may need to add a few tablespoonfuls of water if the balsamic vinegar evaporates away. To test if the onions are ready, pierce the middle of the thickest one with a small knife – it should meet with little resistance. Spoon the syrupy glaze over the onions and serve warm.

RHUBARB CREME BRULEE

66 Crème brûlée was one of the first desserts I learnt to perfect while working under Guy Savoy in Paris. I like to add different flavours to this classic French custard and rhubarb is one of my favourites. Chopped rhubarb is sautéed with honey and vanilla then baked under the creamy custard. As it cooks gently in the oven, the softened rhubarb infuses with the creamy custard to delicious effect. 99

6 servings

20g butter
200g rhubarb, trimmed and chopped
4 tbsp honey
1 vanilla pod, split
300ml double cream
120ml whole milk
5 large free-range egg yolks
60g caster sugar, plus 2 tbsp to finish
few drops of vanilla extract

TIP If you do not have a blowtorch, briefly place the ramekins under a very hot grill to caramelise the sugar, but be careful not to overheat or the custard may melt.

Heat the oven to 140°C/Gas 1. Stand six ramekins or similar ovenproof dishes in a baking tin.

Melt the butter in a wide frying pan. Add the rhubarb, honey and seeds from the vanilla pod. Cook over a high heat, tossing occasionally, for 5–6 minutes until the rhubarb is soft and slightly caramelised at the edges. Spoon into the ramekins.

Slowly heat the cream and milk together in a saucepan until just coming to the boil. Meanwhile, beat the egg yolks, sugar and vanilla extract together in a bowl with a wooden spoon until evenly blended. Trickle the hot, creamy milk on to the egg mixture, beating constantly, until well combined. Strain the mixture through a fine sieve into a large jug. Skim off any froth from the surface, then pour into the ramekins.

Pour warm water into the baking tin to come halfway up the sides of the ramekins. Bake for about 40–45 minutes until the custards are lightly set. To test, gently shake a ramekin – the custard should still be a little wobbly in the centre. Remove the ramekins from the tin and allow to cool completely, then chill until ready to serve.

For the topping, sprinkle 1 tsp sugar evenly on top of each custard, then wave a cook's blowtorch over the surface until the sugar has caramelised. Serve immediately.

MORE THAN A QUARTER OF PEOPLE DO NOT FIND IT EASY TO COOK A MEAL THAT THE WHOLE FAMILY WILL EAT.

"Since when did everyone start getting so fussy? If children see you eating new dishes, then they might be prepared to try them. But my best advice is to get the kids to join in the cooking."

12 Malaysian curry

A typical Malaysian meal comprises a whole array of dishes and rarely begins with an appetiser. However, to keep the meal easy to prepare, I have focused on a fragrant curry with a couple of accompaniments and chosen to serve a light salad starter. The cool, delicate custard tart rounds off the spicy meal perfectly. This menu serves 6.

Rocket, fennel, watercress & pear salad
Malaysian chicken
+ Coconut rice
+ Stir-fried bok choy
Cardamom custard tart

planning your menu

THE DAY BEFORE...
• Make the curry paste and cook the curry, saving the green beans to add just before serving. Cool, cover and refrigerate.
• Make the pastry for the tart, wrap and place in the fridge.

SEVERAL HOURS IN ADVANCE...
• Bake the pastry case, prepare the filling, then bake the tart. Set aside to cool.

AN HOUR AHEAD...
• Take the curry out of the fridge. Prepare the green beans, ready to add.
• For the starter, prepare the fennel shavings and immerse in cold water. Wash the salad leaves. Make the vinaigrette too.

HALF AN HOUR AHEAD...
• Reheat the curry in the oven at 180°C/Gas 4.
• Prepare the bok choy and have the flavouring ingredients ready.
• Cook the coconut rice.
• Drain the fennel and pat dry, toss with the salad leaves.

JUST BEFORE SERVING...
• Assemble the salad starter and serve.
• Keep the curry warm and rest the rice while you eat the starter.
• Stir-fry the bok choy, fluff up the rice and serve the main course.
• Cut the tart into neat slices and serve.

ROCKET, FENNEL, WATERCRESS & PEAR SALAD

"This is a truly refreshing salad with added crunch from the fennel, a peppery kick from the rocket and watercress, and sweetness from the pears. A good choice to precede a curry, it would also make an ideal starter before rich meats like duck, game or pork. The salad is also lovely topped with a scattering of Parmesan shavings."

6 servings

1 large fennel bulb, trimmed
1 large, ripe Comice pear
125g watercress, stems removed
100g wild rocket leaves

HONEY MUSTARD VINAIGRETTE:
1 tbsp wholegrain mustard
1 tbsp Dijon mustard
1 tbsp runny honey
1 tbsp lemon juice
   (or white wine vinegar)
4 tbsp extra virgin olive oil
sea salt and freshly ground black pepper

Cut the fennel into very thin slices, using a mandolin if possible. Plunge the fennel slices into a bowl of iced water and leave for 15–20 minutes to crisp up the leaves.

For the vinaigrette, combine all the ingredients in a screw-topped jar and shake to combine, seasoning to taste with salt and pepper. (Or whisk together in a bowl.) Set aside.

When ready to serve, drain the fennel, pat dry with a clean tea towel and put into a large bowl. Quarter, core and thinly slice the pear, then add to the bowl with the watercress and rocket. Drizzle over the vinaigrette, toss to combine, then pile the salad on to individual plates. Serve immediately.

MALAYSIAN CHICKEN

" For a laid-back Sunday lunch, serve up a curry and coconut rice – with or without a beer in hand. Curries generally improve in flavour the longer you leave them to stand, so make this the day before, leaving just the rice and veggies to cook at the last minute. Traditionally, Malaysian chicken curry includes potatoes but I'm adding green beans instead – for colour and a lighter meal. "

6 servings

CURRY PASTE:

5 garlic cloves, peeled and roughly chopped

4–5 long, red chillies, trimmed, deseeded and roughly chopped

3 lemongrass stalks, trimmed, outer leaves removed and thinly sliced

5cm piece fresh root ginger, peeled and chopped

4 large shallots, peeled and chopped

1 tsp ground turmeric

2–3 tbsp groundnut oil

CURRY:

1kg skinless and boneless chicken thighs

2 tbsp groundnut oil

2 onions, peeled and thinly sliced

sea salt and freshly ground black pepper

4 kaffir lime leaves

1 cinnamon stick

3 star anise

400ml coconut milk

100ml Chicken stock (see page 246)

1 tsp palm sugar (or soft brown sugar)

2 tbsp light soy sauce

2 tbsp fish sauce

400g green beans, trimmed and cut into 5cm lengths

handful of coriander leaves, roughly torn

First make the curry paste. Put the
garlic, chillies, lemongrass, ginger, shallots and turmeric in a food processor and whiz to a paste. With the motor running, trickle in the groundnut oil and blend well, scraping the sides of the processor several times. (Or you can pound the ingredients together in batches using a pestle and mortar.)

To make the curry, cut the chicken into bite-
sized pieces. Heat the groundnut oil in a large cast-iron casserole or heavy-based pan. Tip in the curry paste and stir over a medium heat for a few minutes until fragrant. Add the onions and cook, stirring frequently, for 5 minutes until they are beginning to soften.

Season the chicken pieces with salt
and pepper. Add to the pan and stir to coat them in the spice paste. Add the lime leaves, cinnamon stick, star anise, coconut milk, stock, sugar, soy and fish sauces and bring to the boil. Reduce the heat to a simmer and cook gently for 30–40 minutes until the chicken is tender.

Skim off any excess oil on the surface of
the curry. Taste and adjust the seasoning. Tip in the green beans, put the lid on and cook for another 3–4 minutes until the beans are tender. Scatter the coriander leaves over the curry and serve with coconut rice and stir-fried bok choy.

Coconut rice

Rinse the rice, drain and tip into a heavy-based pan. Add the rest of the ingredients with 200ml water, stir well and bring to the boil, then reduce the heat to a simmer. Cover and gently simmer for 10 minutes. Take off the heat and leave to stand, still covered, for 5–10 minutes. Discard the ginger, fluff the rice with a fork and serve while still hot.

6 servings

350g jasmine, Thai fragrant or other long-grain rice
200ml coconut milk
5cm piece fresh root ginger, peeled
pinch of sea salt

Stir-fried bok choy

6 servings

600g bok choy, washed
3 tbsp groundnut oil
4 garlic cloves, peeled and thinly sliced
2 tbsp light soy sauce
2 tbsp oyster sauce
freshly ground black pepper
sesame oil, to drizzle

Separate the bok choy leaves and stems, then slice the stems on the diagonal. Heat the groundnut oil in a large frying pan or wok until hot. Add the garlic and fry until it turns golden at the edges. Tip in the bok choy stems and stir-fry for a minute, then add the leaves together with the soy sauce, oyster sauce and some black pepper. As soon as the leaves have wilted, transfer the vegetables to a warm plate and drizzle with a little sesame oil to serve.

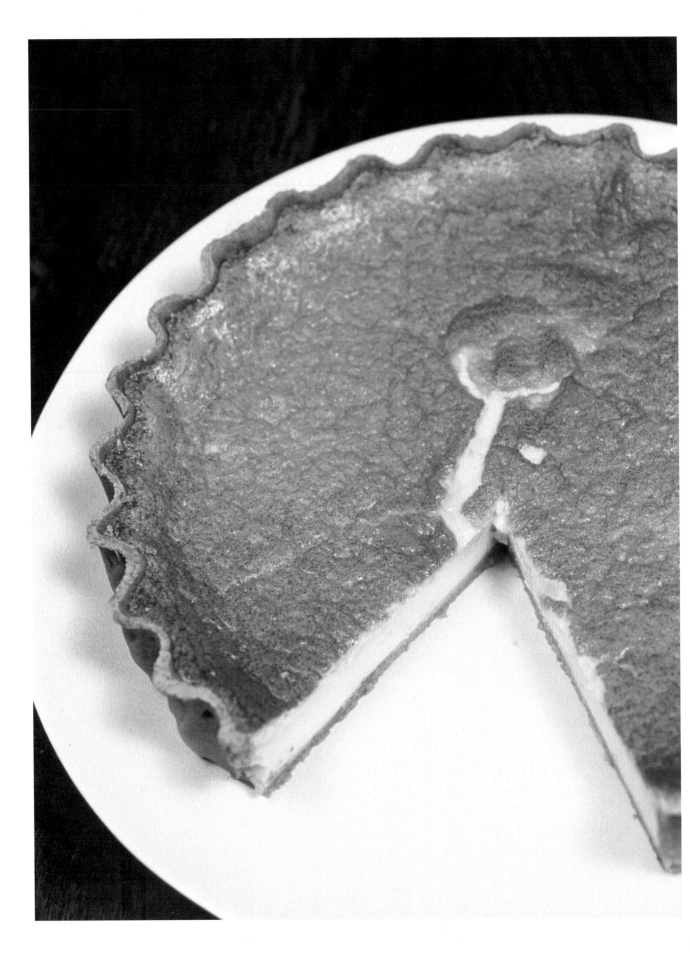

CARDAMOM CUSTARD TART

"This delicious, light custard tart is infused with the subtle and warming flavours of cardamom and cinnamon. It is baked in a low oven until softly set – the custard filling will continue to firm up as it cools."

5–8 servings

300g Sweet flan pastry (see
  page 249)
flour, to dust
600ml whole milk
8 cardamom pods, lightly crushed
1 cinnamon stick
100g caster sugar
1½ tbsp cornflour
4 eggs, separated

Roll out the pastry thinly on a lightly floured surface and use to line a 23cm fluted flan tin, about 5cm deep, with a removable base. Leave the excess pastry overhanging the sides. Press the pastry well into the sides of the tin and pinch together or patch any gaps. Stand the flan tin on a baking sheet. Line the pastry case with foil or baking parchment and baking beans and leave to rest in the fridge for 20 minutes. Meanwhile, heat the oven to 200°C/Gas 6.

For the filling, pour the milk into a pan and add the cardamom and cinnamon. Bring just to the boil, then remove from the heat and leave to stand for 15 minutes to allow the flavours to infuse.

Bake the pastry case 'blind' for about 15 minutes, until the pastry is just set. Remove the foil and beans, then return to the oven for 5 minutes to cook the base. Turn the oven down to 180°C/Gas 4.

In a large bowl, mix together the sugar, cornflour and egg yolks. Strain the milk through a fine sieve into a jug and discard the spices. Gradually stir the infused milk into the egg mixture. Whisk the egg whites until softly stiff and fold into the egg yolk mixture.

Pour the filling into the pastry case. Bake for about 20 minutes until the filling is brown on top, then turn the oven down to 110°C/Gas ½ and bake for a further 1 hour until the custard has just set. It should have a slight wobble in the centre. Trim off the excess crust from the pastry and leave to cool completely before serving.

5 ways with...ONIONS

Stuffed onions
Serves 6

Heat the oven to 200°C/Gas 6. Peel and trim the root ends of 6 large onions, then slice off the top third to expose the layers. Blanch them in a pan of simmering salted water for 15–20 minutes until tender. Drain and refresh under cold running water. With a small spoon, scoop out the inner layers of each onion, leaving the outer two layers intact. Reserve the scooped-out onion flesh.

Fry 2 finely chopped bacon rashers with a little olive oil until golden brown and crisp. Drain on kitchen paper. Whiz 4 slices of crustless white bread and a handful of flat leaf parsley in a food processor to fine crumbs. Take out 2–3 tbsp of the herbed breadcrumbs and set aside. Add the reserved onion flesh to the processor and pulse gently to keep a coarse texture. Mix in half the Parmesan and season well. Toss the rest of the Parmesan with the reserved breadcrumbs.

Spoon the filling into the onions. Stand them on an oiled baking tray and sprinkle with the breadcrumb mixture. Drizzle over a little olive oil and bake for 35–40 minutes or until the topping is golden and crisp. Serve with roast chicken, pork or beef.

Braised leeks
Serves 4–6

Trim 6 large leeks and slice the white part into 5cm lengths (saving the green parts for stock). Melt 30g butter in a heavy-based pan and add the leeks, salt, pepper and 4 tbsp vegetable stock (or water). Bring the liquid to a low simmer and cover the pan with a lid. Braise for about 30–40 minutes until the leeks are tender. Transfer the leeks to a serving dish with a slotted spoon; keep warm. Boil the braising liquor to reduce and thicken, then pour over the leeks. Scatter over some chopped parsley and serve. Goes well with most fish and meat dishes.

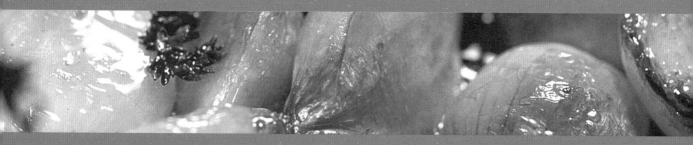

Caramelised shallots with thyme
Serves 4

Put 500g shallots in a heavy-based pan with a little olive oil, a few thyme sprigs, some seasoning and a splash of water. Cook the shallots for about 15–20 minutes until tender, then increase the heat to cook off the liquid and caramelise the shallots. Serve as a garnish to roast pork, beef or poultry dishes.

Spring onion & wild rice salad
Serves 4–6

Put 500g cooked wild rice (or mixed leftover long-grain rice and wild rice) in a bowl. Add 1 finely chopped red pepper, 1 finely chopped red onion, 5–6 finely sliced spring onions and 50g toasted pine nuts or sliced almonds. Toss to mix. For the dressing, whisk together 1 tbsp Dijon mustard, 1 tbsp lemon juice, 1 tbsp runny honey and 4 tbsp olive oil in a small bowl. Drizzle over the salad and toss to mix. Season to taste and serve at room temperature. A perfect side dish for a barbecue or a picnic.

Deep-fried onion rings
Serves 4

Peel 1 large Spanish onion and slice into rings. Season 2–3 tbsp plain flour with salt and pepper, then toss the sliced onions in the flour to coat. Sift 80g self-raising flour into a bowl and make a well in the middle. Add 1 medium egg yolk and gradually beat in 150ml cold water to make a smooth batter. Whisk 2 medium egg whites in another bowl until softly peaking, then fold into the batter.

Heat enough groundnut oil for deep-frying in a suitable pan to 180°C. (A bread cube dropped in should brown in 20 seconds.) Have a tray lined with kitchen paper ready. In batches, dip the onion rings in the batter and deep-fry for 3–4 minutes until golden and crisp. Drain on kitchen paper and sprinkle lightly with sea salt. Add a dusting of mild paprika if you wish, and serve immediately. A great accompaniment to steaks, sandwiches or fried fish in batter.

121

13 Salmon in a parcel

This is ideal for a Sunday lunch – easy to prepare, elegant and full of enticing aromas as you cut into it! Instead of the foie gras starter – you could always serve some little Parmesan puffs (see page 239) and olives with pre-lunch drinks. This menu serves 4–6.

Pan-seared foie gras with Puy lentils

Salmon en croûte
+ Minted hollandaise
+ Creamed leeks
+ Braised cos lettuce

Roasted rhubarb crumble

(see page 239)

planning your menu

A FEW DAYS AHEAD
• Order the foie gras from the butcher (arranging to collect it a day ahead, or fresh on the day if you can).

SEVERAL HOURS IN ADVANCE...
• For the main course, make the pastry; wrap and chill.
• Make the crumble topping. Sauté the rhubarb and allow to cool.

TWO HOURS IN ADVANCE...
• Prepare the spiced filling for the salmon, sandwich the fillets together, wrap in cling film and chill.
• Prepare the leeks and lettuce ready for cooking.

ABOUT AN HOUR AHEAD...
• Wrap the salmon in the pastry; chill.
• Cook the lentils, dress with the vinaigrette; keep warm.
• Assemble the crumble. Prepare the flavoured mascarpone.
• Put the salmon parcel into the oven 15 minutes before you start the meal. Bake the crumble at the same time in a second oven (or bake it before the salmon).
• Make the hollandaise; keep warm.

JUST BEFORE SERVING...
• Pan-fry the foie gras, plate the starter and serve.
• Rest the salmon parcel while you cook the leeks and lettuce.
• Slice the salmon and serve the main course. Let the crumble stand, meanwhile.
• Serve the crumble with the mascarpone.

PAN-SEARED FOIE GRAS WITH PUY LENTILS

❝ Foie gras may be the ultimate indulgence, but few people muster the courage to cook it. It's not difficult but you do need to handle the livers with care or it may prove to be an expensive disaster. Buy fresh foie gras from a good butcher and keep chilled as it deteriorates quickly. Foie gras also cooks quickly, so make sure the lentils are warm and ready to go before you sear it in a hot non-stick pan (without oil). **❞**

4–6 servings

500–600g foie gras, deveined and cut
  into 4 thick, even slices
sea salt and freshly ground black pepper

LENTILS:
250g Puy lentils, rinsed and drained
1 thyme sprig
1 bay leaf
1 garlic clove, peeled and crushed
100g bacon trimmings
  (or 5 rashers of unsmoked bacon)
20g butter
1 carrot, peeled and finely diced
1 celery stalk, finely diced
1 leek, trimmed and finely diced
75g bacon lardons, diced
handful of chives, finely chopped
3 tbsp olive oil
1 tbsp white wine vinegar

First, cook the lentils.
Put them in a saucepan with the thyme, bay leaf, garlic and bacon trimmings and add cold water to cover. Bring to the boil and cook for about 25 minutes until the lentils are tender. Remove the herbs and bacon, drain the lentils and set aside.

Melt the butter
in another pan and add the carrot, celery and leek. Sweat the vegetables for 10 minutes until softened, stirring frequently. In a non-stick pan, fry the bacon lardons until crispy. Add to the lentils along with the chives and vegetables.

Mix the olive oil
and wine vinegar together to make a vinaigrette and season with salt and pepper to taste. Pour two-thirds of the vinaigrette over the lentils, toss well, taste and adjust the seasoning. Keep warm.

Heat a dry frying pan
(preferably non-stick) until you can feel the heat rising from the pan. Quickly fry each slice of foie gras until golden brown but soft in the centre, seasoning as you cook. It should only take 1–2 minutes each side.

Slice the foie gras
in half horizontally. Pile the lentils on to warm plates and top with the foie gras. Drizzle the rest of the vinaigrette around the plates.

TIP The vegetables and bacon lardons add a depth of flavour to the lentils, but you can omit them for a more straightforward dish.

SALMON EN CROUTE

" This dish is based on a classic recipe. Thick sides of salmon are sandwiched with currants and spiced butter, then encased in pastry – here we're using shortcrust as a change from the more typical puff pastry. Remember to leave the salmon to rest for a few minutes after baking before cutting. "

4–6 servings

2 thick salmon fillets, about 500g each, skinned
a little olive oil
60g unsalted butter, at room temperature
finely grated zest of 1 lemon
1 tbsp finely chopped crystallised stem ginger
75g currants
½ tsp freshly grated nutmeg
½ tsp ground cloves
sea salt and freshly ground black pepper
1kg Shortcrust pastry (see page 249)
flour, to dust
2 egg yolks, beaten
few thyme sprigs

TIP To help keep the pastry dry and crisp, you could wrap a layer of fine crêpes (see page 249) around the salmon before enclosing in the pastry.

Check the salmon fillets for small pin bones, removing any that you find with tweezers. Line a baking tray with a lightly oiled piece of foil.

For the filling, mix the butter with the lemon zest, ginger, currants and ground spices. Pat the salmon fillets dry with kitchen paper, then season lightly with salt and pepper. Spread the butter mix over one fillet, on the boned side, then sandwich the two salmon fillets together, in opposite directions so both ends are of an even thickness.

Roll out the pastry thinly on a lightly floured surface to a rectangle, the thickness of a £1 coin. Put the salmon parcel in the centre and brush the surrounding pastry with egg. Bring up the edges, trimming off any excess, and tuck them in before folding the rest of the pastry over to form a neat parcel. Turn the whole thing over so that the seam is sitting on the bottom, and place on the prepared baking tray.

Brush the pastry with the beaten egg. Lightly score the pastry to show 6–8 portions, then lightly score a herringbone or cross hatch pattern to decorate. Sprinkle with sea salt and pepper, and place the thyme sprigs on top. Chill for 15 minutes.

Heat the oven to 200°C/Gas 6. Bake the salmon for 20–25 minutes, depending on the thickness of the salmon. To test if ready, insert a skewer into the middle. It should feel warm for medium cooked salmon. A piping hot skewer indicates that the fish is well done.

Rest the salmon for 5 minutes, then slice thickly. Serve warm, with the minted hollandaise and accompaniments.

Minted hollandaise

4–6 servings
3 tbsp white wine vinegar
½ tsp coriander seeds, finely crushed
6 egg yolks
175ml light olive oil
2 tbsp mint leaves, finely shredded
juice of ½ lemon
sea salt and freshly ground black pepper

Put the wine vinegar and crushed coriander seeds into a small pan. Boil until reduced by half. Place the egg yolks in a bain-marie (or a bowl set over a pan of barely simmering water). Immediately strain the vinegar through a sieve on to the yolks, whisking constantly until the mixture is pale, frothy and doubled in volume. Remove the bowl from the heat and drizzle in the olive oil, whisking constantly. Add the mint, lemon juice and season with salt and pepper. Cover and leave at room temperature until ready to serve.

Creamed leeks

Thinly slice the leeks. Heat the olive oil and butter in a frying pan. Add the leeks and season with a touch of salt and the curry powder. Sweat over a medium heat for 4–5 minutes until tender, stirring occasionally. Stir in the cream and heat through. Serve warm.

4–6 servings
3 leeks, trimmed
1 tbsp olive oil
15g butter
sea salt
1 tsp curry powder
150ml double cream

Braised cos lettuce

4–6 servings
2–3 medium cos lettuce, trimmed
a little olive oil, for cooking
sea salt and freshly ground black pepper
few thyme sprigs
1 tbsp butter
150ml vegetable stock

Slice the lettuce in half lengthways. Heat the olive oil in a large frying pan, add the lettuce, cut side down, and fry for 1–2 minutes until lightly caramelised. Season with salt and pepper. Add the thyme and butter then pour in the stock. Bring to a simmer, cover and gently braise for 4–5 minutes until the lettuce is tender. Lift the lettuce from the stock with a slotted spoon and serve immediately.

ROASTED RHUBARB CRUMBLE

"At the height of its early season, pink rhubarb is an intense pink colour, which gives this crumble filling an enticing look. I sauté the rhubarb to enhance the flavour, add a bit of Japanese pickled ginger to give it warmth, and use vanilla-infused sugar to lend a sweet aroma."

4–6 servings

800g pink rhubarb, trimmed
150g vanilla sugar (see tip)
few knobs of butter
20g Japanese pickled ginger, finely
   chopped

CRUMBLE TOPPING:
150g toasted, skinless hazelnuts
100g plain flour
50g unsalted butter, chilled and cut into
   small cubes
50g demerara sugar
pinch of freshly grated nutmeg
40g porridge oats

TO SERVE:
finely grated zest of ½ lemon
200g mascarpone

TIP To make your own vanilla sugar, simply stick 3 vanilla pods into a 500g jar of caster sugar and leave for a few days to allow the flavour to infuse. Vanilla pods that have been used (ie had their seeds extracted) are fine for this; indeed it is a good way to make full use of expensive vanilla pods.

Heat the oven to 190°C/Gas 5. Cut the rhubarb stalks into 4–5cm lengths. Wash if necessary and pat dry in a clean tea towel.

Toss the rhubarb in the vanilla sugar. Heat a heavy-based sauté pan, then tip in the fruit and add 2 tbsp water. Add a few knobs of butter to enrich the flavour and leave to cook for a couple of minutes. Turn the rhubarb using a thin metal spoon or spatula so the fruit stays intact as far as possible; it should not become too pulpy. Continue cooking for a further 3–5 minutes until the pieces feel just tender when pierced with the tip of a knife. Stir in the ginger, remove from the heat and leave to cool.

Meanwhile, make the crumble. Put the hazelnuts into a large bowl and lightly crush with the end of a rolling pin. With the tips of your fingers, rub the flour and butter together in another bowl until they form a crumb-like mixture. Tip in the demerara sugar, grated nutmeg, oats and hazelnuts. Mix well.

Lay the fruit in a 1.5–2 litre baking dish, then scatter the crumble topping evenly over the top. Bake for 20–25 minutes until the topping is nicely browned. Leave to stand for about 10 minutes. Meanwhile, mix the lemon zest into the mascarpone. Serve the rhubarb crumble warm, with a dollop of the flavoured mascarpone.

14 Surf 'n' turf

Full of zesty flavours, this is a vibrant, colourful menu. A tangy tomato dressing enlivens pan-fried steaks and a tangy mango salsa complements fresh crabmeat. For a more straightforward starter, simply serve the crab mix on chicory leaves with lime wedges on the side, omitting the salsa. This menu serves 6.

Crab wraps with mango salsa

Sirloin steak with tomato tarragon dressing

* Oven chips

Lemon tart

THE DAY BEFORE...
• Make the pastry for the tart, wrap in cling film and refrigerate.

SEVERAL HOURS IN ADVANCE...
• Prepare the crab mix, lettuce and salsa for the starter, but don't add the mango or mint at this stage.
• Make the lemon tart, bake and set aside to cool.
• Make the tomato dressing for the steak, but don't add the herbs.

TWO HOURS AHEAD...
• Take the steaks out of the fridge.
• Peel the potatoes, cut the chips and blanch them, then refresh, drain well and toss in oil to coat.

TWENTY MINUTES AHEAD...
• Bake the chips.
• Make the crab wraps.

JUST BEFORE SERVING...
• Toss the mango and mint into the salsa and assemble the starter.
• Add the herbs to the tomato and tarragon dressing.
• Pan-fry the steaks and rest while you eat the starter (or afterwards if you prefer).
• Slice the steaks and serve with the dressing and chips.
• Dust the tart with icing sugar and slice to serve.

CRAB WRAPS WITH MANGO SALSA

❝ Sweet, crunchy Iceberg lettuce leaves are the 'wraps' for this refreshing, zingy starter. All the components – the crab filling, lettuce leaves and salsa ingredients – can be prepared in advance, to be assembled easily just before serving. To keep the mango fresh and vibrant, however, I suggest you add it to the other salsa ingredients with the mint – at the last minute. ❞

6 servings

300g white crabmeat
½ red chilli, deseeded and very finely diced
1 shallot, peeled and very finely diced
small handful of coriander, leaves chopped
1 tbsp wholegrain mustard
6–7 tbsp Mayonnaise (see page 247)
sea salt and freshly ground black pepper
squeeze of lime juice
1 large head of Iceberg lettuce, washed

SALSA:
1 red chilli, deseeded and very finely diced
1 small red onion, peeled and very finely diced
juice of 1 lime
1 tbsp sesame oil
1 tbsp olive oil, plus extra to drizzle
2 large ripe mangoes, peeled and cubed
handful of mint leaves, shredded

Put the crabmeat
into a bowl and run your fingers through the meat to pick out any little bits of shell. Add the chilli, shallot and coriander and fork through to mix. Stir the mustard into the mayonnaise, then mix enough into the crabmeat to bind the mixture. Season with salt and pepper and add lime juice to taste.

For the salsa,
combine all the ingredients except the mangoes and mint in a bowl. Season lightly with salt and pepper.

Separate the lettuce
into leaves, then trim the sides to give 10–12cm wide strips. Carefully flatten the trimmed lettuce leaves on a chopping board, without tearing them. Place a heaped tablespoonful of crab filling along one end of each strip and roll the lettuce leaf around the filling to encase it. Place, seam side down, on a plate. Continue until you've used all the crab filling.

When ready to serve,
stir the chopped mangoes and shredded mint into the salsa and spoon on to a serving plate. Arrange the crab wraps on top. Drizzle a little olive oil over the wraps and sprinkle with sea salt and pepper. Serve immediately.

SIRLOIN STEAK WITH TOMATO TARRAGON DRESSING

" This is a healthier version of steak and chips, with the traditional béarnaise sauce replaced by a tomato tarragon dressing and lower fat oven chips. The dressing is one of my favourite sauces to serve with steak. It is so quick and easy – the ingredients are simply thrown together. Start cooking the steaks 10 minutes before the chips will be ready. "

6 servings

olive oil, for cooking
6 sirloin steaks, 200–250g each
sea salt and freshly ground black pepper
few knobs of butter

TOMATO TARRAGON DRESSING:
6 medium tomatoes
5 tbsp tomato ketchup
2 tbsp Worcestershire sauce
1–2 tbsp Dijon (or wholegrain) mustard
few dashes of Tabasco
juice of 1 lemon
2 tbsp balsamic vinegar
2 tbsp olive oil
2 large shallots, peeled and chopped
large handful of tarragon, leaves chopped
handful of parsley, leaves chopped

First, make the dressing.
Halve the tomatoes, squeeze out the seeds, then finely chop the flesh and place in a bowl. Add the rest of the ingredients, except the herbs, and season with salt and pepper to taste. Set aside.

Heat a frying pan
with a little olive oil until hot. Season the steaks with salt and pepper. Sear them in the hot pan in batches for 1–1½ minutes on each side, depending on thickness. Add a few knobs of butter to the pan during cooking and spoon the melted butter over the steaks to baste them. When ready, they will feel springy if lightly pressed.

Transfer the steaks
to a warm plate, lightly cover with foil and leave to rest in a warm place for 5–10 minutes. Meanwhile, stir the chopped tarragon and parsley into the tomato dressing.

Slice the steaks
thickly on the diagonal, arrange on warm plates and spoon over the tomato tarragon dressing. Serve with the hot oven chips on the side.

Oven chips

Heat the oven
to 200°C/Gas 6. Peel the potatoes and cut into 1cm thick sticks. Blanch in a pan of boiling salted water for 3 minutes. Drain well and pat dry with a clean tea towel. Spread the chips out on an oiled baking tray. Drizzle with oil, season generously with salt and scatter over the rosemary. Cook in the oven for about 30–40 minutes until golden brown and crisp, turning the potatoes several times during cooking to ensure even colouring.

6 servings

1kg large Desirée potatoes
sea salt
groundnut oil, to oil and drizzle
few rosemary sprigs, leaves only

134

LEMON TART

> " A good lemon tart was once the hallmark of a great pastry chef and the tart featured on the menus of all fine restaurants. The secret is to bake the tart in a very low oven to prevent the lemon custard filling from bubbling and cracking as it sets. The custard will firm up as it cools. "

6–8 servings

300g Sweet flan pastry (see page 249)
flour, to dust
2 large eggs
4 large egg yolks
180g caster sugar
200ml double cream
juice of 2 lemons
icing sugar, to dust
crème fraîche, to serve

TIP For a professional finish, run a cook's blowtorch over the surface to caramelise the icing sugar and give the tart a 'crème brûlée' effect, as illustrated.

Roll out the pastry on a lightly floured surface
and use to line a 20cm tart tin with a removable base. Leave the excess pastry overhanging the sides. Rest in the fridge for 20 minutes.

Heat the oven to 190°C/Gas 5. Line the pastry with
foil or baking parchment and fill with baking beans. Bake 'blind' for 15 minutes – the sides should just begin to colour. Remove the beans and foil, then bake for another 5 minutes until the pastry base is cooked and lightly golden. Lower the oven setting to 110°C/Gas ½.

Whisk the eggs, egg yolks and sugar together in a
bowl, then stir in the cream. Finally add the lemon juice (this will thicken the cream). Strain the lemon filling through a fine sieve into a large jug.

Pour half the filling into the pastry case.
Place the tin on the bottom shelf of the oven. Pull out the shelf halfway, keeping the tin level, and pour in the remaining lemon filling. Carefully push the shelf back into the oven and bake for 50–60 minutes until the filling is almost set. It should have a slight wobble in the centre. Carefully trim the pastry level to the top of the tin and leave to cool completely.

Dust the tart liberally with icing sugar. Cut neat slices
with a warm knife and serve on its own or with some crème fraîche.

NEARLY HALF OF ALL FAMILIES NEVER SIT DOWN FOR A DAILY MEAL TOGETHER.

" It's what the dining room table was invented for ...eating together as a family is really important to me and I am determined to get families back around the table together. **"**

15 Italian essence

I love the simplicity of this menu – chicken braised in Marsala with pan-fried chicory, a creamy saffron-scented soup and an easy, prepare-ahead dessert to finish. It works equally well as a hassle-free Sunday lunch or smart supper. This menu serves 4.

Saffron & cauliflower soup
Chicken Marsala with red chicory
Coffee & chocolate mousse cups

THE DAY BEFORE...
• Prepare the mousse cups and chill.

TWO HOURS IN ADVANCE...
• Joint the chicken and bring to room temperature.

FROM AN HOUR AHEAD...
• Make the soup, saving the garnish to prepare at the last moment.
• Trim and separate the chicory, ready to cook.

ABOUT 15 MINUTES AHEAD...
• Prepare the garnish for the soup.
• Sauté the chicken and add the Marsala.

JUST BEFORE SERVING...
• Gently reheat the soup and serve with the cauliflower garnish.
• Leave the chicken to braise while you have the starter.
• Sauté the chicory and serve the main course.
• Top the mousses with cream, decorate and serve.

SAFFRON & CAULIFLOWER SOUP

" Cooking cauliflower in a poaching liquid of chicken stock and milk helps to keep it pale and velvety, while saffron delicately enhances its flavour. The island of Sardinia is renowned for its saffron and the spice features in Italian cooking. **"**

4 servings

500ml Chicken (or vegetable) stock (see page 246)
500ml milk
2 pinches of saffron strands
sea salt and freshly ground black pepper
1 large cauliflower, cut into florets
25g butter
2 tbsp chopped parsley
olive oil, to drizzle

Pour the stock and milk into a large saucepan and add a pinch of saffron and a generous pinch of salt. Bring to the boil, add the cauliflower florets and lower the heat to a simmer. Cook for about 5–8 minutes until the cauliflower is just tender when pierced with a skewer.

Using a slotted spoon, take out one-quarter of the cauliflower florets and set aside. Put the rest into a blender, add enough of the poaching liquid to half-fill the blender and whiz to a very smooth purée. (Do this in two batches if you need to.)

Return the purée to the pan and add enough of the remaining poaching liquid to obtain a soup consistency. Add another pinch of saffron and reheat gently, seasoning to taste with salt and pepper. Stir in more liquid if the soup is too thick.

Melt the butter in a pan until it begins to foam, then add the reserved cauliflower and sauté for a few minutes until golden brown. Toss in half the chopped parsley and fry until crisp.

Place the cauliflower florets and parsley in the centre of four soup bowls, then pour in the soup, to one side. Serve immediately, topped with a drizzle of olive oil, a sprinkling of parsley and a grinding of black pepper.

143

CHICKEN MARSALA WITH RED CHICORY

" An old Italian favourite, traditionally chicken breasts (or veal escalopes) are pounded into thin escalopes, dredged in seasoned flour, browned and then cooked with Marsala wine. I prefer to brown the chicken pieces whole, to keep them juicy and succulent, and then braise them with a generous amount of Marsala. "

4 servings

olive oil, for cooking
few thyme sprigs
½ head of garlic (unpeeled), cut
   horizontally
1 large chicken, jointed into 8 pieces
sea salt and freshly ground black pepper
½ bottle of Marsala (375ml)
handful of flat leaf parsley, leaves roughly
   chopped

PAN-FRIED RED CHICORY:
4 heads of red chicory, trimmed
olive oil, for cooking
sea salt and freshly ground black pepper

Heat a thin film of olive oil
in a wide frying pan. Add the thyme and garlic and cook gently for a minute. Season the chicken pieces with salt and pepper and add them to the pan, skin side down. Fry for 4–5 minutes until golden brown, then turn the chicken pieces over and cook on the other side for 3–4 minutes. (You may need to brown the chicken in batches if your pan is not wide enough.)

Pour in the Marsala
and stand well back as it may flambé. Lower the heat and braise the chicken for 10–15 minutes until cooked through. To test, pierce the thickest part of a chicken thigh and press lightly – the juices should run clear.

Separate the chicory
into individual leaves. Heat a frying pan with a thin layer of olive oil. Add the chicory leaves, season with a little salt and pepper and toss over a high heat for 1–2 minutes to slightly wilt the leaves. They should still have a slight bite to them.

Pile the chicken
on to a large platter and arrange the sautéed chicory leaves around. Spoon over the Marsala sauce and serve immediately, with a sprinkling of chopped parsley.

144

COFFEE & CHOCOLATE MOUSSE CUPS

" This is a delicious, no-bake mocha dessert that uses mascarpone rather than eggs as a base for the mousse. Do make the espresso strong – the coffee flavour needs to hold up against the chocolate. If you don't have an espresso maker, get a double espresso takeaway from your nearest coffee shop! **"**

4 servings

100g good-quality dark chocolate
  (about 60–65% cocoa solids)
125g mascarpone
2 tbsp icing sugar
4 tbsp strong espresso coffee, cooled
150ml double cream

TO FINISH:
4 tbsp double cream
a little dark grated chocolate
few amaretti biscuits, crushed

TIP To melt the chocolate in a microwave, break into small pieces and tip into a bowl. Microwave on high for a minute, give the pieces a stir, then microwave again for another minute. Stir the chocolate until smooth. This method is only suitable for plain or dark chocolate. White chocolate, in particular, is likely to seize as it overheats in the microwave.

Break the chocolate into small pieces and melt in a heatproof bowl set over a pan of barely simmering water. Stir until smooth, then remove the bowl from the heat and leave to cool.

With a hand whisk, beat the mascarpone and icing sugar together until smooth, then whisk in the espresso and the melted chocolate.

In another bowl, whip the double cream until soft peaks form. Fold the cream into the mocha mixture until well combined. Spoon the mousse into four cappuccino cups or ramekins and chill overnight.

Just before serving, lightly whip the 4 tbsp double cream until thick and swirl over of the mousses. Sprinkle the grated chocolate and crushed amaretti on top and serve immediately.

16 Wild food

This menu brings together some of the great flavours of autumn – wild mushrooms, game, figs and almonds. For a lighter, faster starter, you could omit the pasta and simply pile the mushrooms on to warm toasted baguette slices to serve as bruschetta. This menu serves 4.

Tagliatelle of wild mushrooms

Venison with red wine & chocolate sauce
+ Creamed cabbage & celeriac with pancetta
+ Gratin dauphinoise

Fig & frangipane tart

planning your menu

A DAY IN ADVANCE...
• Make the pasta and keep well wrapped in the fridge.

ABOUT TWO HOURS AHEAD...
• Cut the tagliatelle and keep covered, ready to cook later.
• Take the venison out of the fridge to bring to room temperature.
• Make the sauce for the venison, but don't add the vinegar or chocolate yet.
• Prepare the gratin dauphinoise.
• For the starter, prepare the mushrooms and flavouring ingredients, ready to cook.
• Make the frangipane for the tarts.

AN HOUR IN ADVANCE...
• Shape the pastry discs, place on a baking sheet and chill.
• Shred the cabbage and immerse in cold water. Sweat the root vegetables; set aside.
• Bake the potatoes dauphinoise.
• Prepare the figs and assemble the tarts ready to bake.

JUST BEFORE SERVING...
• Cook the pasta and mushrooms.
• Sear the venison and put in the oven to finish cooking while you have the starter.
• Drain the cabbage.
• Rest the venison.
• Put the fig tarts into the oven to bake.
• Finish the sauce and cabbage, plate the main course and serve.
• Glaze the tarts and leave to stand for 5 minutes before serving.

TAGLIATELLE OF WILD MUSHROOMS

"Fresh pasta soaks up the lovely, earthy flavours of wild mushrooms to delicious effect. When they're not in season, use chestnut mushrooms and a good handful of dried ceps. Soak the dried mushrooms in the usual way, reducing the soaking liquid with a touch of cream to create a flavourful sauce for the pasta."

4 servings

PASTA:
275g Italian '00' flour or strong flour,
   plus extra to dust
pinch of fine sea salt
2 whole eggs
3 egg yolks
1 tbsp olive oil

MUSHROOMS:
500g mixed wild mushrooms
   (such as ceps, girolles, trompettes,
   mousserons), cleaned and trimmed
2 shallots, peeled and finely chopped
1 garlic clove, peeled and crushed
1–2 tbsp olive oil, plus extra to drizzle
sea salt and freshly ground black pepper
few flat leaf parsley sprigs, chopped
small handful of chives, chopped
handful of rocket leaves

TO SERVE:
Parmesan shavings

To make the pasta

put the ingredients into a food processor and whiz until the mixture resembles coarse crumbs. Tip into a bowl and knead together to form a dough. Turn on to a lightly floured surface and knead for a few minutes until the dough is smooth and elastic. Wrap in cling film and rest for at least half an hour.

Cut the dough

into two pieces and work with one at the time, keeping the other piece covered with cling film. Roll out the dough thinly and feed through the pasta machine on its widest setting several times. Now adjust the setting by one notch each time you pass the pasta through, gradually rolling out the pasta more thinly until it is about 1mm thick. Hang the pasta to dry over the back of a clean chair while you roll the rest of the dough.

Pass the pasta sheets

through the machine with the tagliatelle cutters fitted or cut them by hand – the tagliatelle should be about 1cm wide. Lift the noodles from one end, dust lightly with flour to prevent them sticking, and twirl them into a nest on a tray. Repeat with the rest of the pasta.

Halve or slice

larger mushrooms; leave small ones whole. In a pan, sauté the shallots and garlic in olive oil until lightly browned, then add the mushrooms and fry for a few minutes. Season well and add the chopped parsley, chives and rocket towards the end.

Cook the tagliatelle

in boiling salted water for 1½–2 minutes until *al dente*. Drain the pasta and toss quickly with a little olive oil in a hot pan. Tip the mushroom mixture on top and toss well. Season again and add a little more olive oil if necessary. Serve topped with fresh Parmesan shavings.

151

VENISON WITH RED WINE & CHOCOLATE SAUCE

“ Venison is a sumptuous, lean red meat with little saturated fat and cholesterol – great for anyone keeping an eye on calories. It is not uncommon to pair venison with red wine and chocolate – a little grated chocolate whisked into the red wine sauce helps to thicken and enrich it. Do use good quality brown stock – ideally homemade – you won't get the correct consistency for the sauce if you resort to stock cubes. ”

4 servings

150g smoked bacon lardons
250g shallots (about 4 large ones), peeled and roughly chopped
few thyme sprigs
2 bay leaves
1 tsp black peppercorns, crushed
olive oil, for cooking
350ml red wine
1 litre brown Chicken stock (see page 246)
sea salt and freshly ground black pepper
4 venison fillets, about 150g each, trimmed
1 tsp raspberry vinegar
20g bitter chocolate, grated

Sauté the lardons
and shallots with the herbs and crushed peppercorns in a little olive oil, using a wide saucepan, for about 6–8 minutes until the shallots have softened. Add the red wine and boil for 10 minutes until reduced by half. Add the chicken stock and keep boiling until reduced to a syrupy consistency. This may take up to 20–25 minutes. Pass through a sieve into a clean pan, taste and adjust the seasoning.

Heat the oven
to 220°C/Gas 7. Heat an ovenproof frying pan on the hob and add a little olive oil. Season the venison fillets and brown them in the hot pan, allowing 3–4 minutes each side. Remove the pan from the heat and wrap the venison with foil to help retain the moisture. Put the pan into the oven and cook for 6–8 minutes, turning the fillets halfway through. Allow to rest in a warm place for 5 minutes or so.

While the meat rests,
add the raspberry vinegar to the sauce and reheat gently. Take the pan off the heat and whisk in the grated chocolate until it melts and the sauce is smooth. (If it turns grainy, just pass through a fine sieve and it should become smooth again.) Taste and adjust the seasoning.

Slice the venison
and arrange on warm plates. Pour the sauce around and serve immediately, with the accompaniments.

Creamed cabbage & celeriac with pancetta

Heat a little olive oil in a large, wide pan and fry the chopped bacon until golden brown. Add the carrots and celeriac and sweat the vegetables for 6–8 minutes until softened. Add the butter and stir the cabbage through. Cook for 3–4 minutes until the cabbage is tender. Pour in the cream and simmer to reduce slightly. Season generously with salt and pepper and serve.

4 servings

olive oil, for cooking

100g streaky bacon (about 8 rashers), chopped

400g carrots (2–3 large ones), peeled and diced

½ celeriac, peeled and diced

50g unsalted butter

1 small Savoy cabbage, trimmed and finely shredded

200ml double cream

sea salt and freshly ground black pepper

Gratin dauphinoise

4–6 servings

a little olive oil, to drizzle

200ml whole milk

200ml double cream

1 bay leaf

1 garlic clove, peeled and smashed

1 kg waxy potatoes, such as Desirée or Charlotte

200g medium Cheddar, grated

sea salt and freshly ground black pepper

Heat the oven to 200°C/Gas 6. Lightly oil a deep gratin dish. Put the milk, cream, bay leaf and garlic in a pan and heat until simmering. When the liquid begins to bubble up the sides of the pan, turn off the heat and leave to cool slightly.

Peel and finely slice the potatoes, using a mandolin. Scatter one-third of the cheese over the bottom of a baking dish and cover with a layer of the potato slices, overlapping them slightly. Season generously with salt and pepper. Continue layering until you've used up all the cheese and potatoes, seasoning the layers and finishing with cheese. Strain the creamy milk, discarding the bay leaf and garlic. Pour over the potatoes to come two-thirds up the sides (you may not need all of it). Gently press the potatoes down to help them absorb the liquid. Sprinkle with a little more cheese and bake for 35–40 minutes or until the potatoes are golden brown and tender when prodded with a sharp knife. Leave to stand for a few minutes before serving.

FIG & FRANGIPANE TART

66 These beautiful individual tarts make the most of that classic Mediterranean combination of honeyed figs and almonds. For a sumptuous finish, serve them with mascarpone laced with a splash of amaretto or sweet dessert wine. 99

Makes 4–6

500g ready-made puff pastry
flour, to dust
1 egg yolk, beaten, to glaze
10–12 ripe figs

FRANGIPANE:
100g butter, softened to room
  temperature
100g icing sugar, plus extra to dust
1 large egg, beaten
100g ground almonds
25g plain flour

TO SERVE:
runny honey, to drizzle
double cream, to serve

TIP If you can only find unripe figs in your local supermarket, leave them in the fruit bowl next to a bunch of bananas to encourage the ripening process.

First make the frangipane. Cream the butter and icing sugar together in a bowl, then slowly add the egg, mixing until it is fully incorporated. Add the ground almonds and flour and fold through until evenly combined. Leave the mixture to rest for about 5 minutes. Heat the oven to 200°C/Gas 6.

Roll out the puff pastry thinly on a lightly floured surface until it is the thickness of a £1 coin. Using a small plate or saucer as a guide, cut out 4–6 rounds from the pastry. Score a 1cm border around the edge of each circle, making sure you don't cut right through the pastry. Lift the circles on to a large baking tray and glaze the border with the egg yolk. Smooth a thin layer of frangipane over the centre of each pastry round.

Slice two figs horizontally into rounds. Cut the rest of the figs into wedges. Arrange on top of the frangipane like a flower, with a fig round in the centre surrounded by fig wedges. Dust with a little icing sugar and bake until the pastry is crisp and golden, about 20 minutes. The pastry border will puff up around the fig flowers.

While still warm, drizzle honey over the figs and frangipane to glaze. Cool slightly before serving, with cream.

"Fish is one of the most delicious and nutritious foods available to us. Fishmongers, sadly, are now few and far between, but if you've got one near you, treasure it. Always check fish and shellfish carefully for quality and freshness before you buy. Remember, fish is such an easy thing to cook that it's perfect for a hassle-free lunch."

17 Fast food

An effortless meal that needs little planning or advance preparation. To make it even more straightforward, you could omit the starter and instead serve a simple antipasti spread of Italian cured meats, tomatoes, olives and artichoke hearts. This menu serves 4.

Baby squid in tomato sauce with chard
Griddled spring chicken & vegetables on focaccia
Iced berries with white chocolate sauce

planning your menu

SEVERAL HOURS (OR A DAY) AHEAD...
- Put the chicken to marinate.
- Freeze the berries.

TWO HOURS IN ADVANCE...
- Prepare the ingredients for the starter, ready to cook.

30 MINUTES AHEAD...
- Make the white chocolate sauce and keep warm.
- Braise the squid and blanch the chard for the starter; refresh in cold water.

JUST BEFORE SERVING...
- Cook the chicken, vegetables and focaccia on the griddle; keep warm in a low oven.
- Sauté the chard, assemble the starter and serve.
- Plate the main course, add the dressing and serve.
- Divide the frozen berries among plates and pour the warm chocolate sauce over as you serve.

BABY SQUID IN TOMATO SAUCE WITH CHARD

" An Italian friend who grew up in Tuscany described this rustic dish to me and I was fascinated by the clever pairing of fish with Swiss chard. The tender braised squid really benefits from the succulent chard leaves and the flavours are held together with white wine, garlic and chilli. This dish would also make a delicious light lunch, served with a rustic Italian loaf or some pasta. "

4 servings

2–3 tbsp olive oil
1 shallot, peeled and finely chopped
1 celery stalk, trimmed and finely chopped
1 leek, trimmed and finely chopped
3 garlic cloves, peeled and finely chopped
500g baby squid, cleaned and cut into rings
sea salt and freshly ground black pepper
100ml dry white wine
4 ripe plum tomatoes, quartered

SAUTEED CHARD:
1 large Swiss chard, about 750g, washed and trimmed
2–3 tbsp olive oil
2 garlic cloves, peeled and chopped
½ red chilli, deseeded and chopped

Heat the olive oil in a large heavy-based pan and add the shallot, celery, leek and garlic. Stir over a medium heat for 6–8 minutes until the vegetables are soft and translucent.

Add the squid and season well with salt and pepper. Cook for a few minutes, then pour in the white wine. Lower the heat and gently braise the squid for about 10–15 minutes until tender. Tip in the quartered tomatoes and cook over a medium heat for another 5 minutes. Keep warm.

Coarsely chop the Swiss chard in the meantime, separating the stems and leaves into two piles. Heat the olive oil in a large pan and gently sauté the garlic and chilli until the garlic turns golden. Meanwhile, blanch the chard stems in a pan of boiling salted water for 4–5 minutes, then add the leaves and cook for another minute. Drain well. Add the chard to the garlic and chilli and toss over a medium heat for a few minutes until the stems are tender. Season generously with salt and pepper.

As soon as it's ready, divide the chard among warm plates, add the braised squid and serve.

GRIDDLED SPRING CHICKEN & VEGETABLES ON FOCACCIA

This is quick and easy to cook on the griddle and when the weather turns warm you can take it outside to barbecue. If you have time, marinate the chicken pieces in the olive oil overnight to allow the flavours of the garlic and rosemary to infuse.

4 servings

2 spring chickens or poussins, about
   450g each
few rosemary sprigs, leaves only
3–4 garlic cloves, halved, with skin on
olive oil, to drizzle
sea salt and freshly ground black pepper
2 large courgettes, trimmed
1 small aubergine, trimmed
1 large yellow pepper
1 large red pepper
few thyme sprigs
1 large (or 2 medium) focaccia loaves

BALSAMIC DRESSING:
6 tbsp olive oil
3 tbsp balsamic vinegar

TIP If you are cooking this dish for a larger crowd, I suggest you poach the chicken pieces for about 10 minutes in advance. This reduces the time needed for griddling and makes it easier to ensure all the chicken is cooked through.

Carve out the chicken breasts and legs (or get your butcher to do this). Put them into a large bowl with the rosemary and 2 garlic cloves. Drizzle generously with olive oil and season well with pepper. Set aside to marinate.

Cut the courgettes into 1cm thick rounds. Slice the aubergine into rounds of a similar thickness. Halve, core and deseed the peppers, then cut into wedges. Place the vegetables in a bowl, add the remaining garlic and thyme and toss with a generous drizzle of olive oil. Season with salt and pepper.

For the dressing, mix the olive oil and balsamic vinegar together and season with salt and pepper to taste. Set aside.

Heat a griddle pan until almost smoking. Using tongs, place the vegetables on the griddle and cook for about 6–8 minutes, turning them halfway through cooking. Remove to a plate and set aside.

Season the chicken with salt and cook on the griddle, allowing about 3–4 minutes each side for the breasts, 5–6 minutes each side for the legs. Check it is cooked through – the meat will be firm and the juices should run clear when the thickest part is pierced with a skewer. Transfer to a plate and keep warm.

Cut the focaccia into four 10–12cm squares. If very thick, slice them in half horizontally. Griddle for 20 seconds on each side to warm through – watch closely as they burn easily. Brush with a little olive oil if you wish and place on warm plates.

Spoon the griddled veg on to the bread and top each serving with a chicken breast and leg. Spoon over the balsamic dressing and serve immediately.

ICED BERRIES WITH WHITE CHOCOLATE SAUCE

"This must be the easiest pudding to prepare. Simply freeze a selection of berries overnight and pour over some melted white chocolate to serve. The berries will start to thaw as soon as they come in contact with the warm chocolate sauce."

4 servings

125g blueberries
125g raspberries
125g blackberries
125g redcurrants
125g strawberries, hulled and quartered
200g white chocolate

TIP It is important to cut any larger berries, such as strawberries, into even-sized pieces to ensure that all the fruit defrosts at the same rate when you pour the sauce on.

Arrange the fruit in a shallow freezer container or on a baking tray and freeze for at least 2 hours or overnight until solid.

Break the chocolate into small pieces and place in a bowl set over a pan of barely simmering water, making sure the bowl isn't in direct contact with the water. Allow the chocolate to melt slowly, stirring occasionally, until smooth. Pour the melted chocolate into a warm small serving jug. If not serving immediately, keep the chocolate sauce warm by sitting the jug in a pan of hot water.

Divide the frozen berries among four chilled serving plates. Drizzle the warm chocolate sauce over the fruit at the table.

MORE THAN HALF OF ALL HOUSEHOLDS WATCH THE TV WHEN EATING TOGETHER.

"Switch the television off at mealtimes. You don't need that going on when you're trying to talk to your friends and family. Mealtimes are about savouring the food on your plate, appreciating it and taking your time over it. You don't need any extras with that."

18 Quick & easy

I love the rustic flavours here, especially the combination of tastes and textures in the salad and the peasant-style main dish. The entire three-course meal can be rustled up in next to no time – Sunday lunch has never been easier! This menu serves 4.

Vine tomato & bread salad

Italian sausages with lentils

Lemon posset

planning your menu

THE DAY BEFORE...
• Make the dessert and refrigerate (or prepare on the day at least 3 hours ahead).

HALF AN HOUR AHEAD...
• Start cooking the lentils.
• Prepare the salad starter and leave to stand.
• Cook the sausages and combine with the lentils; keep warm.

JUST BEFORE SERVING...
• Finish the salad and serve.
• Take the lemon possets out of the fridge and set aside at room temperature.
• Serve up the sausages and lentils.
• Serve the lemon possets.

168

VINE TOMATO & BREAD SALAD

" Italians often make this salad as a way of using up stale or 'day-old' bread – they call it *panzanella*. The bread brilliantly soaks up the sweet and tangy juices from the tomatoes and the extra virgin olive oil. We used ciabatta rolls, but any good rustic bread will do. "

4 servings

6–8 slices of leftover bread
6 large ripe vine tomatoes
1 red onion, peeled and thinly sliced
juice of ½ lime
6 tbsp extra virgin olive oil
sea salt and freshly ground black pepper
pinch of caster sugar (optional)
handful of flat leaf parsley

TIP As the intention of the dish is to use up leftover bread, there is no need for precision – use whatever type or amount of bread you have to hand and adjust the tomatoes and dressing according to taste.

Tear the bread into bite-sized pieces and place in a large bowl. Cut the tomatoes into wedges and add them to the bowl with the red onion. Drizzle with the lime juice and olive oil. Season with salt and pepper, then toss well. Leave to stand for 15 minutes to allow the flavours to mingle together.

Taste and adjust the seasoning, adding a little more lime juice if you prefer a sharper taste, or a pinch of sugar if the salad is too tart.

Tear the leaves from the parsley and toss them with the salad just before serving.

171

ITALIAN SAUSAGES WITH LENTILS

" In Italy, sausages are served with lentils as part of a traditional New Year's meal, rather than something you would resort to for a fry-up. I think they make the ideal Sunday lunch – quick, easy and very tasty. Try to get good quality sausages, such as Genovese, from an Italian deli and use the right kind of lentils that will hold their shape after cooking – ideally little brown Castelluccio lentils from Umbria or French Puy lentils. "

4 servings

olive oil, for cooking
200g smoked bacon lardons
1 onion, peeled and finely chopped
1 medium carrot, peeled and cut into
   1cm cubes
3 bay leaves
500g Castelluccio or Puy lentils, rinsed
   and drained
sea salt and freshly ground black pepper
1 large garlic clove, peeled and smashed
12 Italian sausages
100ml dry white wine
handful of flat leaf parsley, leaves
   chopped

Heat a little olive oil
in a heavy-based saucepan and fry the lardons until lightly golden, about 5 minutes. Add the onion, carrot and bay leaves, stir well and cook over a medium heat for 5–6 minutes until the onions begin to soften.

Tip in the lentils,
stir well and pour in enough water to cover. Bring to the boil, lower the heat and simmer, covered, for 25–30 minutes until most of the liquid has been absorbed and the lentils are tender. Season generously with salt and pepper.

Cook the sausages
in the meantime. Heat a little olive oil in a heavy-based frying pan. Add the garlic and cook for a minute. Add the sausages and pan-fry for about 5 minutes, turning occasionally, until lightly golden. Deglaze the pan with the white wine and bring to the boil. Lower the heat to a simmer, and leave the sausages to braise for 15–20 minutes until cooked through.

With a pair of tongs,
transfer the sausages to the lentils, nestling them among the vegetables and lentils and adding the pan juices. Reheat for a few more minutes.

Divide the lentils and sausages
among warm shallow bowls. Sprinkle generously with chopped parsley and a grinding of black pepper, then serve.

172

LEMON POSSET

Lemon posset is delightfully simple, tangy and very rich, so a little goes a long way. We serve it in shot glasses with long, thin biscuits on the side for dipping. To make a lighter dessert, you could fold through some Italian meringue to aerate the dense lemon cream.

4 servings

300ml double cream
75g caster sugar
juice of 1–2 lemons
langues de chats or almond biscuits,
  to serve

Pour the cream
into a small saucepan and add the sugar. Slowly bring to the boil, stirring constantly to dissolve the sugar. Once it comes to the boil, let the cream bubble for a further 3 minutes, stirring all the time.

Remove the pan
from the heat and pour in the juice of 1 lemon, stirring the mixture thoroughly as you do so. It should start to thicken instantly. Taste the mixture and add a little more lemon juice if it's not tart enough. The posset should be sweet, tangy and creamy.

Allow to cool
for about 5 minutes, then pour into individual glasses. Cover with cling film and chill in the refrigerator for at least 3 hours or overnight. If the possets are very firm, take them out of the refrigerator 15 minutes before serving to soften. Serve with dessert biscuits.

5 ways with...GREENS

Braised kale with pancetta
Serves 4

Trim and chop 500g kale. Fry 150g chopped pancetta with 2 tbsp olive oil in a large pan until golden brown. Stir in the chopped kale, add 100ml chicken or vegetable stock and season well. Cook over a high heat for a few minutes, stirring frequently, until the kale is wilted and tender. Taste and adjust the seasoning, then serve. Delicious with poultry, fish or meat dishes.

Sautéed spinach with nutmeg
Serves 4–6

Heat 2 tbsp olive oil in a large pan. Tip in 600g washed baby leaf spinach leaves and stir over a high heat until just wilted. (You may need to cook the spinach in two batches if your pan is not wide enough.) Season with salt, pepper and a little grated nutmeg and serve immediately. An excellent base for fish, vegetarian or beef dishes.

Cavolo nero with garlic & chilli
Serves 4–6

Remove the stems from 2 bunches of cavolo nero and finely shred the leaves. Heat 2 tbsp olive oil in a large pan and gently fry 1 thinly sliced medium onion and 2 thinly sliced garlic cloves until the onions begin to soften. Stir in 1 finely chopped, deseeded red chilli and cook for another minute. Add the cavolo nero and sauté for 4–5 minutes or until wilted. Season generously with salt and pepper and serve immediately. A great side dish to Italian-style fish, chicken, veal or pork dishes.

176

Purple sprouting broccoli with pine nuts & sesame seeds
Serves 4–6

Trim 750–1kg purple sprouting broccoli and cut into 5cm lengths. Blanch in a pan of boiling salted water for a couple of minutes until *al dente*, then refresh under cold running water and drain well. Heat 3–4 tbsp olive oil in a large pan and add a couple of knobs of butter. Toss in the broccoli, warm through and season with salt and pepper to taste. Finally toss in 2 tbsp toasted pine nuts and 1–2 tbsp toasted sesame seeds. Serve warm as an accompaniment to chicken, pork or pasta.

Watercress & spinach purée
Serves 4–6

Trim 300g watercress and 100g spinach leaves. Blanch the watercress in a pan of boiling salted water for 5 minutes, then add the spinach leaves and wilt for a minute. Drain in a colander and press with the back of a ladle or spoon to extract as much liquid as possible. For a drier result, wrap in a clean cloth and squeeze out the liquid. Whiz the green pulp in a food processor to a smooth purée, scraping down the sides a few times. With the motor running, pour in 4 tbsp double cream and blend for several minutes until the purée is very smooth. Season to taste with salt and pepper. Use as a garnish for beef or fish dishes.

19 Retro dining

Revive well-loved classics for a nostalgic Sunday lunch that's guaranteed to appeal. Most of the preparation for each course can be done well in advance, leaving you plenty of time to relax with family and friends before the meal. This menu serves 4.

Horseradish marinated salmon

Beef wellington
+ Wilted baby gem lettuce
+ Sautéed potatoes with thyme & garlic

Gordon's trifle

planning your menu

A DAY AHEAD...
• Prepare the marinated salmon and keep well wrapped in the fridge.
• Make the trifle (but not the topping), cover and refrigerate.

SEVERAL HOURS IN ADVANCE...
• Drain the salmon, rinse off marinade and coat in the horseradish cream. Wrap and chill. Make the balsamic dressing too.
• Prepare the beef fillet, wrapping it in the mushroom paste, Parma ham and outer cling film. Refrigerate.

TWO HOURS AHEAD...
• Wrap the beef in the pastry; chill again.
• Peel and parboil the potatoes. Drain and toss in olive oil.
• Prepare the lettuce ready for cooking.
• Make the crème fraîche topping and spread on top of the trifle. Make the peanut brittle and set aside.

AROUND 40 MINUTES AHEAD...
• Glaze the pastry and put the beef wellington in the oven to cook.
• Crush the peanut brittle, ready for the trifle.

ABOUT 15 MINUTES AHEAD...
• Slice the salmon and plate the starter.
• Sauté the potatoes; keep warm.

JUST BEFORE SERVING...
• Dress the salmon and serve.
• Rest the beef while you eat the starter.
• Wilt the lettuce, carve the beef and serve the main course.
• Sprinkle the peanut brittle over the trifle and serve.

FABRICA DE JEAN "LA SUPERIOR"
Artesianas n° 735310
MISTERIOSO
EVERY GARMENT IS GOTTEN UP FOR A SPECIAL PURPOSE AND WE GUARANTEE IT TO PLEASE IN EVERY WAY.
W1

HORSERADISH MARINATED SALMON

" This is similar to curing salmon for gravadlax, though I add some horseradish, which gives it a slight peppery kick. Instead of the balsamic dressing, you could serve mayonnaise spiked with a little horseradish as a creamy sauce on the side. "

4 servings

500g salmon fillet, skinned
25g coarse sea salt
freshly ground black pepper
25g granulated sugar
2–3 tbsp creamed horseradish
large handful of dill, parsley and
  coriander sprigs, chopped

DRESSING:
1 tbsp balsamic vinegar
1 tbsp Dijon mustard
3 tbsp olive oil
sea salt and freshly ground black pepper

Trim the salmon, removing any fins and cutting away any bands of pale fat at the edges. Run your fingers over the fish to check for small bones and use tweezers to remove any you come across.

Mix the salt, pepper and sugar together and rub this mixture all over the salmon. Wrap in cling film, lay in a shallow dish and refrigerate overnight.

Pour away any liquid that exudes from the salmon. Unwrap the fillet and rinse off the marinade, then pat dry with kitchen paper. Brush the skinned side with a thin layer of horseradish cream and coat with the chopped herbs. Wrap tightly in cling film and chill until ready to serve.

Holding the knife at a 45° angle, slice the marinated salmon as thinly as possible. Fan out the salmon slices on individual serving plates.

For the dressing, whisk the balsamic vinegar, mustard and olive oil together and season with salt and pepper to taste. Drizzle over the salmon to serve.

181

BEEF WELLINGTON

This is an impressive dish and one that's easier than it looks. To keep the pastry light and crisp, we wrap the beef and mushrooms in a layer of Parma ham – to shield the pastry from moisture. You could take it further and add a layer of thin crêpes (see page 249).

4 servings

400g flat cap mushrooms, roughly
   chopped
sea salt and freshly ground black pepper
olive oil, for cooking
750g piece of prime beef fillet
1–2 tbsp English mustard
6–8 slices of Parma ham
500g ready-made puff pastry
flour, to dust
2 egg yolks, beaten

Put the mushrooms into a food processor with some seasoning and pulse to a rough paste. Scrape the paste into a pan and cook over high heat for about 10 minutes, tossing frequently, to cook out the moisture from the mushrooms. Spread out on a plate to cool.

Heat a frying pan and add a little olive oil. Season the beef and sear in the hot pan for 30 seconds only on each side. (You don't want to cook it at this stage, just colour it.) Remove the beef from the pan and leave to cool, then brush all over with the mustard.

Lay a sheet of cling film on a work surface and arrange the Parma ham slices on it, in slightly overlapping rows. With a palette knife, spread the mushroom paste over the ham, then place the seared beef fillet in the middle. Keeping a tight hold of the cling film from the edge, neatly roll the Parma ham and mushrooms around the beef to form a tight barrel shape. Twist the ends of the cling film to secure. Chill for 15–20 minutes to allow the beef to set and keep its shape.

Roll out the puff pastry on a floured surface to a large rectangle, the thickness of a £1 coin. Remove the cling film from the beef, then lay in the centre. Brush the surrounding pastry with egg yolk. Fold the ends over, then wrap the pastry around the beef, cutting off any excess. Turn over, so the seam is underneath, and place on a baking sheet. Brush all over the pastry with egg and chill for about 15 minutes to let the pastry rest. Heat the oven to 200°C/Gas 6.

Lightly score the pastry at 1cm intervals and glaze again with beaten egg yolk. Bake for 20 minutes, then lower the oven setting to 180°C/Gas 4 and cook for another 15 minutes. Allow to rest for 10–15 minutes before slicing and serving with the accompaniments. The beef should still be pink in the centre when you serve it.

Wilted baby gem lettuce

Take the larger leaves from the lettuce (saving the smaller innermost ones for salads). Heat a little olive oil in a pan. Add the lettuce leaves and quickly sauté with a sprinkling of salt and pepper over a high heat just enough to wilt them – less than a minute. Serve at once.

4 servings

2 large baby gem lettuce, trimmed
a little olive oil, for cooking
sea salt and freshly ground black pepper

Sautéed potatoes with thyme & garlic

4 servings

8 large Charlotte potatoes, about 500g in total, peeled
sea salt and freshly ground black pepper
olive oil, for cooking
1 head of garlic (unpeeled), halved horizontally
1 thyme sprig

Parboil the potatoes in salted water for 10–12 minutes. Drain well and quarter lengthways. Heat a little olive oil in a frying pan. Sauté the potatoes with the garlic and thyme until golden brown, crisp on the outside and cooked through. Remove the thyme and garlic, season well and serve.

GORDON'S TRIFLE

" With the right combination of textures and flavours, a trifle can be very tempting. We vary the fruit between the layers of liqueur-soaked sponge and vanilla custard according to the season. To top it off, a sprinkling of crushed, salted peanut brittle balances out the sweetness and adds crunch. "

4–6 servings

CUSTARD:
400ml milk
120ml double cream
1 vanilla pod, split
6 egg yolks
60g caster sugar
1 tbsp cornflour

TRIFLE:
2 tbsp muscovado sugar
4 peaches, stoned and sliced
  into wedges
few knobs of unsalted butter
4–5 tbsp Grand Marnier, or to
  taste
1 large jam-filled Swiss roll, cut
  into 1cm slices

TOPPING:
2x 200g tubs of crème fraîche
1 tbsp muscovado sugar
1 vanilla pod, split
oil, to oil
2 tbsp caster sugar
100g salted peanuts (or unsalted
  if you prefer)

To make the custard, put the milk and cream into a heavy-based saucepan with the seeds from the vanilla pod. Heat gently to infuse. In a large bowl, whisk together the egg yolks, sugar and cornflour. When the cream begins to bubble up the sides of the pan, take off the heat and slowly pour on to the eggs, whisking all the time. Pour through a fine sieve back into the hot pan. Return to a medium-low heat and keep whisking until the custard thickens. Set aside to cool.

For the trifle, melt the muscovado sugar in a wide non-stick pan over a medium heat, swirling it around as it begins to caramelise. Add the peaches, toss to mix and allow to take on a little colour before adding a few knobs of butter. Sprinkle with 2 tbsp Grand Marnier and let bubble until the liqueur has reduced right down and the fruit is tender, but retaining its shape. Leave to cool.

Line the bottom of a large serving bowl with the Swiss roll slices and drizzle with 2–3 tbsp Grand Marnier. Spoon the caramelised fruit on top, followed by the custard. Cover the bowl with cling film and chill for least 2 hours or overnight (the longer the better).

For the topping, mix the crème fraîche with the muscovado sugar. Add the seeds from the vanilla pod and stir until evenly combined. Spread on top of the trifle and refrigerate while you prepare the peanut brittle. Have ready a lightly oiled baking sheet. Toss the caster sugar and peanuts in a dry non-stick pan over a high heat to caramelise the sugar and toast the peanuts. When the caramel turns golden brown, tip the mixture on to the baking sheet in a single layer. Leave to cool and set, then crush roughly in a large bowl with the end of a rolling pin.

Just before serving, scatter the peanut brittle evenly over the top of the trifle.

185

20 Sole food

Savour the fabulous aromas that this easy-to-prepare light menu offers and you will return to it time and time again. Sautéed spinach with nutmeg (see page 176) is a good alternative to the red chard accompaniment. This menu serves 4.

Spring garden soup

Sole en papillote

+ Sautéed red chard with garlic

+ Minted new potatoes

Apple tarte fine with rum & raisin ice cream

planning your menu

A FEW DAYS AHEAD
• Order the sole from the fishmonger and ask him to fillet it for you (arranging to collect it a day ahead, or fresh on the day if you can).

THE DAY BEFORE...
• Make the ice cream and freeze.

TWO HOURS AHEAD...
• Prepare the apple purée and refrigerate (or do this the day before).
• Prepare the veg for the soup, set aside.
• Scrub the potatoes and immerse in cold water.
• Prepare the chard so it's ready to cook.
• Shape and bake the pastry discs for the apple tarts.

AN HOUR AHEAD...
• Slice the apples and assemble the tarts; chill.
• Assemble the sole parcels, ready to cook.
• Make the spring garden soup.
• Blanch and refresh the chard so it's ready to cook.
• Bake the tarts for 5 minutes, then cool for 5 minutes.

JUST BEFORE SERVING...
• Ladle the soup into bowls, top with mint and serve.
• Put the sole parcels into the oven and cook the potatoes while you eat the starter.
• Sauté the chard, dress the potatoes and serve the main course.
• Put the apple tarts into the oven to finish baking while you eat the main course.
• Glaze the tarts and serve topped with a scoop of ice cream.

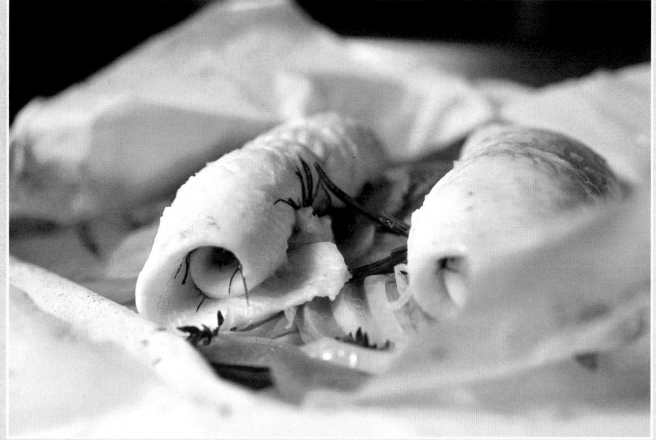

SPRING GARDEN SOUP

66 This colourful soup makes the most of spring vegetables. These are chopped and gently 'sweated' in a little olive oil before any liquid is added to the pan to encourage them to release their natural juices and gives the final broth a full flavour. If you like, you can add a spoonful of grated Parmesan at the end, to thicken the soup slightly and provide extra savouriness. 99

4 servings

150g unsmoked bacon lardons
olive oil, for cooking
1 onion, peeled and chopped
100g baby leeks, trimmed and chopped
100g baby carrots, scrubbed and roughly
  chopped
2 small turnips, about 175g, peeled and
  cut into 1cm cubes
1 large potato, about 150g, peeled and cut
  into 1cm cubes
100g green beans, trimmed and cut into
  2–3cm sticks
¼ Savoy cabbage, cored and chopped
sea salt and freshly ground black pepper
handful of mint leaves, chopped

In a large pan, sauté the lardons in a little olive oil
for 3–4 minutes until lightly golden. Add the onion and leeks and cook
for a few more minutes. Stir in the chopped carrots, turnips and potato.
Cover the pan with a lid and sweat the vegetables for 4–5 minutes until
soft and translucent. Meanwhile, put the kettle on to boil.

Pour boiling water into the pan to cover the
vegetables (about 1.2 litres). Add the green beans and cook for about
2 minutes. Finally throw in the chopped cabbage and simmer for
2 minutes or until it has wilted. Season to taste with salt and pepper.

Ladle the soup into warm bowls and sprinkle with
freshly chopped mint to serve.

SOLE EN PAPILLOTTE

Lemon sole has a soft texture and subtle flavour. It is ideally suited to cooking en papillotte, as the fish gentle steams in the parcel helping to preserve its delicate qualities. Do slice the vegetables thinly as they will need to cook at the same rate as the sole.

4 servings

2 small carrots, peeled
2 small leeks, white part only
3–4 spring onions, trimmed
4–5 garlic cloves (unpeeled), halved
few rosemary sprigs, leaves only
few thyme sprigs
8 skinned lemon sole fillets, about
  150–175g each
sea salt and freshly ground black pepper
few dill sprigs
olive oil, to drizzle
about 100ml dry white wine

Heat the oven to 200°C/Gas 6. Cut out eight large squares of baking parchment, measuring about 30x30cm. Thinly slice the carrots, leeks and spring onions on the diagonal. Tip the vegetables and garlic into a bowl, add the rosemary and thyme and toss to mix. Scatter the mixture in neat piles in the centre of four of the parchment sheets.

Season each sole fillet with salt and pepper and place a few dill sprigs on top. Roll up the fillets, enclosing the dill and place two rolled fillets on each pile of vegetables. Drizzle with olive oil and sprinkle with salt and pepper.

Place another sheet of paper on top of each parcel and using short folds, secure the edges to seal in the fish and vegetables. When you've reached the last fold, carefully pour in a generous splash of white wine and a little water. Seal the parcels and place on one or two large baking sheets. Bake for 20 minutes or until the lemon sole feels firm in the middle.

Lift the parcels on to warm large plates. Bring to the table and cut a cross in the centre of the parchment with kitchen scissors to open the parcels. Accompany with sautéed red chard and minted new potatoes if you wish.

Sautéed red chard with garlic

Roughly chop the chard and separate the stalks from the leaves. Bring a pan of salted water to the boil. Blanch the stalks for 3–5 minutes, then add the leaves and cook for another minute. Refresh under cold running water and drain well. When ready to serve, heat a little olive oil in a pan and add the garlic. When it begins to turn golden, toss in the chard. Season well and cook for 2–3 minutes until the chard is tender. Serve warm.

4 servings

1 large red chard, about 1kg
sea salt and freshly ground black pepper
olive oil, for cooking
3 garlic cloves, peeled and finely chopped

Minted new potatoes

4 servings

500g new potatoes, preferably Jersey Royals, washed
sea salt and freshly ground black pepper
small bunch of mint
3–4 tbsp Classic vinaigrette (see page 247)
finely grated zest of 1 lemon

Scrub the potatoes and cut any larger ones in half. Place in a large saucepan and add cold water to cover. Add a large pinch of salt and the stalks from the bunch of mint. Partially cover with a lid and simmer for 15–20 minutes until the potatoes are just tender when pierced with a skewer. Meanwhile, shred the mint leaves. Drain the potatoes and toss with the vinaigrette, salt and pepper while still warm. Sprinkle with the shredded mint and lemon zest to serve.

APPLE TARTE FINE WITH RUM & RAISIN ICE CREAM

" This classic tart is quite time-consuming to make, but well worth the effort. We contrast our warm apple tarts with homemade rum and raisin (actually sultana) ice cream. To save time, you could just fold some rum-soaked sultanas through a tub of good-quality ready-made vanilla ice cream. "

4–6 servings

RUM AND 'RAISIN' ICE CREAM:
85g golden sultanas
about 100ml white rum
1 quantity Crème anglaise (see page 248)

APPLE PURÉE:
2 medium cooking apples, about 500g
    in total
4 tbsp golden caster sugar, or more
    to taste
¼ tsp ground cinnamon
squeeze of lemon juice

TART:
500g ready-made puff pastry
flour, to dust
3–4 Granny Smith or Braeburn apples
20g unsalted butter, melted, plus extra
    to grease
1–2 tbsp golden caster sugar, to sprinkle
2 tbsp apricot jam, warmed with 1 tbsp
    water

For the ice cream,
put the sultanas and rum into a small pan, bring to the boil, then take off the heat and set aside to soak, preferably overnight. Churn the crème anglaise in an ice cream machine until slushy. Add the sultanas with the rum and continue churning until the ice cream is firm. Transfer to a plastic container and freeze.

For the apple purée,
peel, core and chop the apples. Place in a pan with the sugar, cinnamon, lemon juice and 4 tbsp water. Stir and bring to the boil. Lower the heat, cover and cook gently for 10 minutes or until the apples are soft. Taste and add a little more sugar if the apples are too tart. Push through a fine sieve and leave to cool.

Heat the oven
to 200°C/Gas 6. Roll out the puff pastry thinly on a lightly floured surface to a 2mm thickness. Using a 13cm plate or saucer as a guide, cut out 4–6 rounds and place on two large baking sheets lined with baking parchment. Peel, core and thinly slice the apples.

Spread a thin layer
of apple purée over the pastry discs, leaving a 1–2cm margin. Arrange the apple slices in a circle on top of the purée, overlapping them slightly. Brush them with melted butter and sprinkle with a fine layer of sugar. Chill for 15–20 minutes.

Bake the tarts
for 5 minutes, then leave to cool for 5 minutes. Cover each sheet of tarts with lightly greased baking parchment and weigh down with another baking sheet. Holding the sandwiched baking sheets tightly, flip them so the pastries are on top of the apples. Bake for another 15–20 minutes until the pastry is brown and crisp.

Flip the baking sheets
carefully again as you remove them from the oven. Transfer the tarts to a wire rack and brush with the warm apricot jam to glaze. Serve them warm, with a scoop of ice cream.

5 ways with...CARROTS

Carrot, beetroot & orange salad
Serves 4–6

Peel and grate 500g carrots and 250g cooked beetroot. Put into a bowl with 3 peeled and segmented oranges, a small handful of chives and 4–5 tbsp Classic vinaigrette (see page 247). Quickly toss all the ingredients together, but avoid overmixing. Serve as a barbecue accompaniment or as part of a light starter.

Carrot purée
Serves 4

Peel and thickly slice 750g carrots and cook in boiling salted water for 5–7 minutes or until tender. Drain well, reserving the cooking liquid. Whiz the carrots to a fine purée in a food processor, adding 1–2 tbsp cooking liquor to get them moving and scraping down the sides a few times. For a smooth result, push the purée through a fine sieve. Reheat just before serving, adding a few knobs of butter and seasoning to taste. A tasty base on which to serve chicken breasts or monkfish.

Pan-roasted carrots with gremolata
Serves 4–6

Scrub 750g baby carrots. Melt 30g unsalted butter in a pan, add the carrots with a little salt and pepper and cook over a medium heat, tossing occasionally, until just tender. Meanwhile, to make the gremolata, finely chop a handful of flat parsley leaves and mix with 2 tsp finely crushed garlic, 2 tsp finely grated lemon zest, 2 tbsp olive oil and some seasoning. Scatter the gremolata over the carrots as you serve them. Delicious warm or at room temperature, with lightly spiced fish, chicken or pasta.

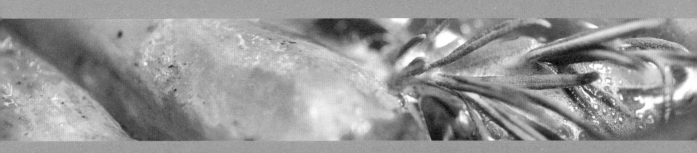

Glazed carrots with rosemary
Serves 4–6

Peel 750g–1kg medium carrots and parboil in salted water for 7–9 minutes. Drain and refresh under cold running water. When ready to serve, melt 30g unsalted butter in a wide sauté pan, add the carrots with a few sprigs of rosemary and toss over a high heat until the carrots are golden and coated in a buttery glaze. Sprinkle with salt and pepper and serve warm. A great accompaniment to roast meats.

Spiced carrots with star anise
Serves 4–6

Peel 1kg medium carrots (about 12), quarter lengthways, then cut into 7–8cm sticks. Melt 30g unsalted butter in a heavy-based pan over a medium heat. When it begins to foam, add the carrot sticks and sauté for 5 minutes until slightly softened. Sprinkle with 2 tbsp soft brown sugar, a squeeze of lemon juice, 4–5 star anise, ¼ tsp ground cinnamon and a pinch of cayenne pepper if you like. Add 120ml water (or vegetable stock) and simmer until the carrots are tender and the liquid is reduced to a syrupy glaze. This may take up to 10 minutes. Season with salt and pepper to taste. Serve with Moroccan-style tagines, casseroles or hearty fish dishes.

Spring into summer with this tantalising menu that offers some captivating flavours – wild garlic, tender, young peas and early strawberries. Pare the meal down to two courses if you like, either leaving off the risotto or crumble. This menu serves 4.

Wild garlic & parsley risotto
Chicken with petits pois à la française
Strawberry, peach & ginger crumble

planning your menu

SEVERAL HOURS IN ADVANCE...
• For the dessert, cook the fruit and allow to cool. Prepare the crumble topping.

AN HOUR AHEAD...
• Cook the chicken and reduce the stock; set aside ready to assemble.
• Prepare the ingredients for the petit pois and sauté the onions; set aside.

30 MINUTES AHEAD...
• Assemble the crumbles, ready to bake.
• Make the risotto.
• Put the crumbles into the oven.
• Add the stock and peas to the pearl onions and leave to simmer gently while you have the starter.

JUST BEFORE SERVING...
• Plate the risotto and serve.
• Return the chicken pieces to the sauce and reheat gently while you finish the petit pois.
• Take the puddings out of the oven and leave to stand.
• Plate the main course and serve.
• Serve the pudding.

WILD GARLIC & PARSLEY RISOTTO

66 Wild garlic is at its best during spring when it is mild-tasting but incredibly fragrant. When you make this risotto, rather than discard the parsley stalks, add them to the hot stock to impart flavour. The chopped parsley leaves should be added right at the end, to keep their vibrant colour. 99

4 servings

1.3 litres Chicken (or vegetable) stock (see page 246)
3 tbsp olive oil, plus extra to drizzle
3–4 wild garlic cloves (or new season's garlic), sliced
4 shallots, peeled and finely chopped
350g risotto rice, such as Carnaroli
sea salt and freshly ground black pepper
few knobs of butter
100g Parmesan, freshly grated, plus shavings to serve
handful of flat leaf parsley, leaves chopped

Bring the stock to a simmer in a saucepan and keep it at a simmer over a low heat.

Heat the olive oil in a larger pan and add the garlic, followed by the shallots. Cook for 2–3 minutes until the shallots have softened. Stir in the rice and cook for a couple of minutes until the rice grains appear translucent, stirring frequently.

A ladleful at a time, add the hot stock to the rice and cook, stirring, until almost all the liquid is absorbed before adding the next ladleful. When you have added most of the stock (you may not need all of it), season and taste the rice. It should be *al dente*, cooked but with a bite in the centre. Take the pan off the heat.

Stir the butter into the risotto, followed by the grated Parmesan and chopped parsley. Add a splash more stock to keep the rice moist and creamy if you like. Serve at once, scattered with Parmesan shavings and topped with a drizzle of olive oil.

CHICKEN WITH PETITS POIS A LA FRANÇAISE

> "My version of a chicken fricassée pairs the tender chicken with sweet, braised peas, rather then a creamy mushroom sauce, for an altogether lighter affair."

4 servings

1 large chicken, about 1.5–2kg
3 tbsp plain flour
sea salt and freshly ground black pepper
2–3 tbsp olive oil
2 carrots, peeled and cut into 1cm cubes
2 celery stalks, cut into 1cm cubes
1 large onion, peeled and finely chopped
2 garlic cloves, peeled and chopped
few thyme sprigs
2 bay leaves
150ml dry white wine
800–900ml Chicken stock (see page 246)
handful of flat leaf parsley, chopped

PETIT POIS A LA FRANÇAISE:
2 tbsp olive oil
150g small pearl onions, peeled
few thyme sprigs
1 bay leaf
100ml Chicken stock (see page 246)
500g young, tender peas, preferably
   fresh (thawed, if frozen)
50g butter, cut into cubes
2 baby gem lettuce, shredded

TIP Chicken breasts take less time to cook than the other pieces. To keep them succulent, take them out after 20 minutes' cooking and warm through in the sauce at the end.

Joint the chicken into eight pieces. Season the flour with salt and pepper and toss the chicken pieces in it to coat all over. Heat a little olive oil in a wide frying pan and fry the chicken pieces, in two batches, over a medium heat until golden brown on all sides. Remove the chicken with a slotted spoon and set aside on a plate.

Add the carrots, celery, onion, garlic, thyme and bay leaves to the pan. Stir and cook over a medium heat for 4–5 minutes until the vegetables are beginning to soften. Pour in the white wine, scraping the bottom of the pan with a wooden spoon to deglaze. Return the chicken pieces to the pan, nestling them among the vegetables, and pour in enough stock to cover. Bring to the boil, then reduce the heat to a low simmer. Skim off any scum that rises to the surface, put the lid on the pan and simmer gently for 30–40 minutes until the chicken is tender.

With a pair of tongs, remove the chicken from the pan and set aside. Strain the stock through a fine sieve, pushing with the back of a wooden spoon to extract as much juice from the vegetables as possible; discard the vegetables. Return the stock to a clean, wide pan. Skim off any excess fat from the top of the liquid, then allow to bubble for 10–15 minutes until reduced and thickened.

Cook the petit pois in the meantime. Heat the olive oil in a large, shallow pan. Add the pearl onions, thyme and bay leaf and sauté over a medium heat for 5 minutes. Add the stock, peas and some salt and pepper. Simmer gently for 10 minutes until the vegetables are tender. Stir in the butter, a few knobs at a time, to enrich and help thicken the sauce. Finally, mix through the lettuce and heat briefly until wilted.

Return the chicken to the pan and reheat gently in the sauce for a few minutes. Serve with the peas and a generous sprinkling of chopped parsley.

STRAWBERRY, PEACH & GINGER CRUMBLE

66 This is another lovely crumble, marrying together the delightful flavours of strawberry, peach and ginger. The great thing about crumbles is that you can make them all year round – using different fruits as they come into season. 99

4 servings

3 ripe peaches
300g strawberries, hulled and quartered
2 pieces of stem ginger in syrup, drained and finely chopped
2 tbsp sugar

CRUMBLE:
50g toasted hazelnuts
70g plain flour
pinch of ground cinnamon
25g cold butter, cut into small pieces
50g demerara sugar
2 tbsp caster sugar

TO SERVE:
pouring cream or Crème anglaise (see page 248)

Heat the oven
to 200°C/Gas 6. Halve, stone and roughly dice the peaches, then put them into a dry non-stick pan with the strawberries, ginger, sugar and 2 tbsp water. Cook over a high heat for 2 minutes until the fruit is slightly softened but not mushy. Tip into a bowl and allow to cool.

For the crumble,
lightly crush the hazelnuts in a bowl with the end of a rolling pin. In a large mixing bowl, stir together the flour and cinnamon. Using the tips of your fingers, rub the butter into the flour until the mixture resembles coarse breadcrumbs. Stir through the crushed hazelnuts and demerara sugar.

Spoon the softened fruit
into four wide ramekins or individual baking dishes. Top with the crumble mixture, scattering it evenly, and stand the dishes on a baking sheet. Bake for 15–20 minutes until the topping is golden brown and crisp.

Leave the crumble
to stand for a few minutes before serving, with cream or crème anglaise.

"The important thing is to try and enjoy cooking. It shouldn't be something that you dread. What is there to be scared of? You only learn through making mistakes so they are not something to be afraid of. I still get it wrong sometimes and I am still learning new things – that doesn't stop and you shouldn't either. Keep going until the fear is gone!"

22 Christmas dinner

I love the magic of Christmas. We usually have a large gathering and I get everyone to join in with the cooking. The traditional turkey is always popular, but I prefer the other courses to be less predictable. If you are unsure about oysters, start with Horseradish marinated salmon (see page 181), a great prepare-ahead recipe. This menu serves 6–8.

Champagne oysters with cucumber pappardelle

Herb buttered turkey with citrus breadcrumbs

+ Golden roasted potatoes + Honey glazed carrots

+ Glazed parsnips + Sautéed Brussels sprouts with almonds

+ Devils on horseback + Cranberry sauce + Pan gravy

Hugh's chestnut & chocolate truffle cake

planning your menu

WELL IN ADVANCE...
• Order your turkey.
• Order oysters from your fishmonger.
• Make the cranberry sauce.

THE DAY BEFORE...
• Prepare the devils on horseback, ready for cooking; keep refrigerated.
• Make the herb butter and prepare the breadcrumbs, ready for sautéeing. In the evening, stuff the turkey; keep chilled.

4 OR 5 HOURS IN ADVANCE...
• Bring the turkey to room temperature.

3 HOURS AHEAD...
• Put the turkey in the oven, remembering to baste it occasionally.
• Shuck the oysters for the starter.
• Prepare all the vegetables. Blanch the sprouts, carrots and parsnips and keep immersed separately in chilled water. Toss the peeled potatoes in oil, ready to roast.

• Make the chestnut and truffle cake (or do this a day ahead if serving cold).
• Make the stock for the gravy.

AN HOUR AHEAD...
• Prepare the ingredients for the starter ready for cooking; keep the cucumber ribbons immersed in chilled water.
• Make the stock for the gravy.

ABOUT 15 MINUTES AHEAD...
• Sauté the breadcrumbs and cook the devils on horseback; keep both warm.
• Put the potatoes in the oven.
• Assemble the starter.

JUST BEFORE SERVING...
• Rest the turkey while eating the starter.
• Finish cooking the carrots, parsnips and sprouts. Finish the gravy.
• Carve the turkey and serve with the accompaniments.
• Unmould the truffle cake and serve.

TIP To shuck oysters, first check that all the oysters are alive by tapping them gently on the surface. They should close tightly – discard any that don't. Hold the oyster using a thick, folded tea towel with one hand and an oyster knife (or a blunt butter knife) in the other. Keeping the oyster level, stick the knife through the hinge of the oyster shell and wriggle it from side to side to cut through the hinge muscle. Push in the knife a little further then twist up to lift the top shell. Tip the oyster juice into a bowl and remove any pieces of shell from the oyster. Slide the knife along the bottom shell to cut through the muscle and release the oyster.

CHAMPAGNE OYSTERS
WITH CUCUMBER PAPPARDELLE

" This refreshing soup makes a great starter before a substantial meal. Do have all the ingredients prepared before you start cooking as the cucumbers and oysters take no time to heat through. Shuck the oysters just before cooking to keep them as fresh as possible and save the juices as they'll be used to season the stock. "

6–8 servings

2 litres good vegetable stock
4 long cucumbers, peeled
24 fresh oysters
juice of ½ lemon
100ml double cream or crème fraîche
4 baby gem lettuce, trimmed and finely
  shredded
handful of chives, chopped
glass of Champagne
sea salt and freshly ground black pepper

Bring the stock to the boil in a large pan. Using a vegetable peeler, peel about 8–10 wide, thin ribbons (resembling pappardelle pasta) from each cucumber, avoiding the seeds in the middle.

Shuck the oysters and add the juices to the hot stock with a little lemon juice and the cream. Allow the liquid to come back to the boil, then add the cucumber ribbons and oysters. Cook for 30 seconds only, then take off the heat and stir in the lettuce and chives. Add the Champagne and check the seasoning.

Pile the cucumber strips into the middle of four warm bowls. Divide the oysters among the bowls and pour in the soup. Serve at once.

HERB BUTTERED TURKEY WITH CITRUS BREADCRUMBS

> 66 It was a treat to raise our own turkeys for Christmas last year, even if it did test Tana's patience at times! It has given us a new meaning to good, organic food. 99

6–8 servings

1 large oven-ready turkey, about 5–5.5kg
sea salt and freshly ground black pepper
2 large onions, peeled and halved
1 orange, halved
1 head of garlic (unpeeled), halved
    horizontally
few bay leaves
few thyme sprigs
olive oil, to drizzle

HERB BUTTER:
small bunch of flat leaf parsley, chopped
small bunch of tarragon, chopped
1 tbsp thyme leaves
250g butter, softened to room
    temperature
1 black truffle (optional)

CITRUS BREADCRUMBS:
½ loaf of day-old bread, about 300g,
    crusts removed
grated zest of 1 orange
grated zest of 1 lemon
olive oil, for cooking
50g pancetta (about 7–8 rashers),
    chopped
½ onion, peeled and finely diced
few thyme sprigs
200g pine nuts
150g butter, cut into cubes
squeeze of lemon juice

For the herb butter, mix the chopped herbs into the softened butter. If using the truffle, finely slice and chop, then mix into the herb butter. Season well and spoon the flavoured butter into a piping bag.

Holding the turkey with one hand and starting from the neck flap, use the fingers of your other hand to loosen the skin over the breasts without tearing the skin. Move your hand towards the lower side of the breast and towards the thighs and separate the skin from the meat. You want to create a large pocket with which to stuff the herb butter. Pipe the butter into the pockets over the breasts and thighs. Gently massage over the skin to spread the herb butter evenly.

Heat the oven to 220°C/Gas 7. Open up the cavity of the turkey, season with salt and pepper and stuff with the onions, orange, garlic, bay leaves and thyme sprigs. Tuck the legs under the neck skin to secure them in place, or tie with kitchen string. Place the turkey, breast side up, in a large roasting tray. Drizzle with a little olive oil and season well. Roast for 10–15 minutes until the skin is crisp and golden. Lower the oven setting to 180°C/Gas 4 and cook for approximately 30 minutes per kg, basting occasionally. To test that your turkey is cooked, skewer the thickest part of the thigh and check that the juices are running clear, not at all pink.

Meanwhile, make the breadcrumbs. Tear the bread roughly and whiz to coarse crumbs in a food processor. Add the orange and lemon zests and season well. Pulse a few times until well mixed. Heat a little olive oil in a large frying pan and fry the pancetta for a minute. Toss in the onion, thyme and pine nuts. Cook for 3–4 minutes before adding the butter around the edge of the pan. Allow the butter to foam and turn a golden brown before adding the breadcrumbs. Mix well and cook, tossing frequently, for 5 minutes until the crumbs are nicely toasted and golden. Squeeze over a little lemon juice, discard the thyme and adjust the seasoning. Keep warm.

When ready, cover the turkey with foil and leave to rest for at least 20 minutes. Carve the breast and thighs and serve with the citrus breadcrumbs, gravy and other accompaniments.

Pan gravy

6–8 servings

2 tbsp vegetable oil
turkey giblets
3 shallots, peeled and chopped
2 bay leaves
few thyme sprigs
6 black peppercorns
1 tbsp plain flour
100ml white wine

Heat the oil in a pan and fry the giblets until browned all over. Pour in 600ml water, stirring to deglaze the pan and add the shallots, bay leaves, thyme and peppercorns. Bring to the boil and skim off any scum from the surface. Lower the heat and simmer for 1 hour. Strain the stock through a fine sieve.

Pour off excess fat from the turkey roasting tray and set it over a medium heat. Stir in the flour and cook for 2 minutes. Gradually whisk in the wine, then the strained stock and simmer for 15 minutes or until thickened to the consistency of single cream. Season to taste.

Golden roasted potatoes

Heat the oven to 220°C/Gas 7. Heat the duck fat or oil in a sturdy baking tray over a medium heat. Add the potatoes with plenty of seasoning and turn until golden and crisp. Put the tray into the oven and roast for 40–45 minutes until the potatoes are cooked through (they should give easily when pierced with a knife). Drain on kitchen paper and serve.

6–8 servings

3–4 tbsp duck fat or vegetable oil
1.5–1.8kg potatoes, such as Charlotte or Desirée, peeled
sea salt and freshly ground black pepper

Sautéed brussels sprouts with almonds

6–8 servings

750g Brussels sprouts, trimmed
sea salt and freshly ground black pepper
few knobs of butter
olive oil, for cooking
75g flaked almonds, toasted

Cook the Brussels sprouts in boiling salted water for 7–9 minutes, until slightly softened. Drain the sprouts, refresh under cold running water and drain thoroughly.

Just before serving, heat a little butter and olive oil in a large sauté pan. Add the sprouts and sauté until tender, scattering over the flaked almonds towards the end of cooking to allow them to brown gently.

Honey glazed carrots

Cook the carrots
in boiling salted water until just tender, about 7–9 minutes. Drain, refresh under cold running water and drain well. Heat the butter in a large sauté pan. Add the carrots, season with salt and pepper, drizzle over the honey and toss well to coat. Sauté until the carrots are well glazed. Serve at once.

6–8 servings

12–16 medium carrots, peeled
sea salt and freshly ground black pepper
50g salted butter
2 tbsp runny honey

Glazed parsnips

6–8 servings

6–8 large parsnips, peeled and halved
lengthways
sea salt and freshly ground black pepper
50g salted butter

Cook the parsnips
in boiling salted water until just tender, about 7–9 minutes. Drain, refresh under cold running water and drain well. Heat the butter in a large sauté pan. Add the parsnips, season and toss well to coat. Sauté until they are caramelised at the edges. Sprinkle with pepper and serve at once.

Devils on horseback

Slice the bacon
in half lengthways, wrap each half around a prune and secure with a cocktail stick. Pan-fry in the olive oil for 3–4 minutes, turning occasionally, until the bacon is crisp and prunes have softened. Remove the cocktail sticks and serve warm.

8 servings

8 rashers of streaky bacon
16 pitted prunes
2 tbsp olive oil

Cranberry sauce

8 servings

grated zest and juice of 1 orange
200g fresh (or frozen) cranberries
100g caster sugar
1 cinnamon stick

Put all the ingredients
in a small saucepan and set over a high heat. Cook for 5–7 minutes until the cranberries start to soften or burst. Transfer to a bowl and leave to cool. If making in advance, pour straight into a sterilised jar, seal while it is still warm and refrigerate when cooled, for up to a week.

213

HUGH'S CHESTNUT & CHOCOLATE TRUFFLE CAKE

66 This cake caused a stir in the kitchen when Sharon Osbourne declared it a winner against my chocolate hazelnut tart! I thought it only fair to readers to include Hugh's recipe in the book and he has kindly given me his blessing to do so. 99

6–8 servings

250g dark chocolate, broken into pieces
250g unsalted butter, plus extra to
  grease
250g peeled, cooked chestnuts
125ml whole milk
125ml single cream
4 large eggs, separated
125g caster sugar

TO SERVE:
mascarpone or crème fraîche, to serve
handful of marrons glacé, chopped
  (optional)

TIP This heavenly cake is also delicious served with whipping cream flavoured with brandy-soaked raisins.

Heat the oven to 170°C/Gas 3. Grease and line a 25cm springform cake tin.

Melt the dark chocolate and butter together in a bain-marie (or a bowl set over a pan of barely simmering water) or directly in a heavy-based pan over a very gentle heat. Take off the heat and cool slightly. In another pan, heat the chestnuts with the milk and cream until just boiling, then whiz to a rough purée in a food processor (or mash thoroughly with a potato masher).

Beat the eggs yolks and caster sugar together until pale and smooth. Stir in the chocolate and the chestnut purée until you have a smooth, blended mixture.

Whisk the egg whites in a clean bowl until stiff. Carefully fold them into the chestnut mixture, then spoon into the prepared tin. Bake for 25–35 minutes until the cake has just set but still has a slight wobble in the middle. Leave to cool a little in the tin to allow it to firm up slightly.

Carefully release the tin and cut the warm cake into slices – it will be soft and mousse-like. Alternatively, leave it to go cold and it will firm up when set.

Slice the truffle cake and serve each portion with a dollop of mascarpone or crème fraîche and a scattering of chopped marrons glacé if you like.

23 Pig roast

This is a celebration of the pig in its different guises – a tasty terrine of ham, followed by two roasts and a refreshing dessert to round off the meal. Serve either pork roast or go the whole hog and cook both! After all, leftovers make great sandwiches. Serves 6–8.

Ham hock persillade with piccalilli
Roast loin of pork with crisp crackling
Pressed belly of pork
+ Caramelised apple wedges
+ Broccoli with red onions, capers & almonds
White chocolate pannacotta with Champagne granita

planning your menu

A FEW DAYS AHEAD...
• Order the meat from your butcher (arranging to collect it a day ahead).
• Make the piccalilli (this can be done well ahead and improves with keeping).

THE DAY BEFORE...
• Make the persillade and refrigerate.
• Prepare the granita and freeze.
• Make the pannacotta and chill.
• Slow-roast the pork belly, press and refrigerate overnight. Make the gravy, cool and chill.

TWO HOURS AHEAD...
• Prepare the pork loin so it is ready for roasting. Set aside at room temperature.

AN HOUR AHEAD...
• Take the pork belly out of the fridge to bring to room temperature.
• Roast the pork loin.
• Prepare the ingredients for the accompaniments, ready to cook.

JUST BEFORE SERVING...
• Unmould the persillade and slice, ready to serve with the piccalilli.
• Cut the pork belly into portions and put into a very hot oven to fast-roast.
• Rest the pork loin while you eat the starter.
• Rest the pork belly while you cook the accompaniments and reheat the gravy.
• Serve the main course.
• Unmould the pannacottas and serve with the granita and raspberries.

216

HAM HOCK PERSILLADE
WITH PICCALILLI

66 When I opened my first restaurant, I couldn't afford to put expensive ingredients or prime meats on the menu. Less popular cuts provided more flavour and better value for money. This cold terrine shows how a humble cut can be elevated to another division with careful cooking. It can also be served as part of a 'posh' ploughman's lunch. **99**

6–8 servings

2 large ham hocks, about 1.2kg each (see tip)
1 tsp coriander seeds
1 tsp black peppercorns
2 bay leaves
few thyme sprigs
2 tbsp small capers, rinsed and drained
50g gherkins, rinsed and finely chopped
handful of flat leaf parsley, finely chopped
sea salt and freshly ground black pepper
2 gelatine leaves

TO SERVE:
Piccalilli (opposite)

TIP I use unsmoked or 'green' ham hocks for this terrine, but you can use smoked hocks if you prefer. Smoked ham hocks will need to be soaked overnight in cold water to remove excess salt.

Put the ham hocks into a large pan and cover with cold water. Bring to the boil and boil steadily for 10 minutes, skimming off the scum that floats to the surface. Remove the hocks and discard the water.

Return the hocks to the rinsed-out pan along with the coriander seeds, peppercorns, bay leaves and thyme. Cover with cold water and bring to a simmer. Allow to simmer gently for 2½–3 hours until the hocks are tender and the flesh flakes easily.

To keep them succulent, leave the hocks to cool in the liquid, then lift them out. Strain the liquor into a clean pan and boil for 10–15 minutes until reduced by half.

Line a 1.5 litre terrine with a double layer of cling film, leaving some excess draping over the sides. Peel off the skin, then flake the ham or cut into small chunks. Put into a large bowl with the capers, gherkins and parsley. Mix well, seasoning with salt and pepper. Pile the mixture into the terrine and pat down evenly.

Soak the gelatine leaves in cold water for a few minutes to soften. Measure 250ml of the reduced stock and season lightly (saving the rest for soup). Squeeze out excess water, then add the gelatine leaves to the hot stock. Stir until dissolved, then pour into the terrine mould to just cover the filling. Gently tap the terrine to ease the stock into any gaps and top up with a little more stock if necessary. Cover with cling film and weigh down with a similar-sized loaf tin (or a carton of milk). Chill overnight or until set.

To unmould the persillade, tug at the cling film. Unwrap the persillade and cut into thick slices. Serve with the piccalilli.

Piccalilli

Dissolve the salt in 1 litre cold water to make a brine, then add the onions, shallots and cauliflower. Top up with a little more water if the brine doesn't cover the vegetables. Give the vegetables a stir and put a plate on top to keep them submerged in the brine. Leave in a cool place overnight.

The next day, drain the vegetables and soak in several changes of cold water to remove excess salt; drain well. Dissolve the sugar in the cider vinegar over a low heat, then boil for 15–20 minutes until reduced by half. Top up with 250ml water and return to the boil. In a bowl, combine the cornflour, mustard, ginger and turmeric. Add 2–3 tbsp of the reduced vinegar and stir to a smooth paste. Whisk this into the rest of the vinegar and simmer for about 5 minutes until the mixture thickens enough to lightly coat the back of a wooden spoon.

Add the vegetables to the vinegar, bring to the boil and simmer for 3 minutes until *al dente*, tender but with a bite. Pack in clean, sterilised kilner jars and seal while still warm. Store in a cool, dark cupboard for up to 1 month and refrigerate after opening. The flavour of the piccalilli improves with keeping.

Makes about 1.5 litres

50g fine sea salt

300g pearl or small pickling onions, peeled

300g shallots, peeled and halved

1 small cauliflower, about 450g, trimmed and cut into small florets

150g caster sugar

500ml cider vinegar

2 tbsp cornflour

2 tbsp dry English mustard

1½ tbsp ground ginger

1½ tbsp ground turmeric

219

ROAST LOIN OF PORK
WITH CRISP CRACKLING

" The secret to perfect crackling is oil, salt and heat. The pork skin is scored, rubbed with olive oil and a generous amount of sea salt, then subject to an initial blast of high heat. The heat is essential to getting the crackling off to a good start. All the pork needs then is a good, slow roast to keep the flesh juicy and succulent. "

6–8 servings

1 pork loin, about 1.3kg
2 garlic cloves, peeled and finely chopped
grated zest of 1 lemon
small handful of flat leaf parsley,
   leaves only
small handful of sage leaves
sea salt and freshly ground black pepper
olive oil, to drizzle

TIP A very sharp, clean Stanley knife (or craft knife) is the most effective tool to use for scoring the tough pork skin.

Heat the oven to its maximum setting, probably 240°C/Gas 9. Score the pork skin in a criss-cross pattern at 2cm intervals. Turn it, so the flesh side is facing upwards, and cut a slit along the side of the loin to open it out like a butterfly. Sprinkle the garlic and lemon zest all over the flesh and scatter the parsley and sage leaves along the centre. Sprinkle with salt and pepper.

Roll up the loin and secure with kitchen string at 3–4cm intervals. Place, skin side up, in a lightly oiled roasting tin. Pat the scored skin dry with kitchen paper, then rub with a generous drizzle of olive oil and a few large pinches of sea salt. Roast for 15–20 minutes until the skin is golden and starting to crisp. Turn the oven down to 180°C/Gas 4 and continue to roast, allowing 25 minutes per 450g, until the pork is cooked through and tender. Rest for 10–15 minutes before carving.

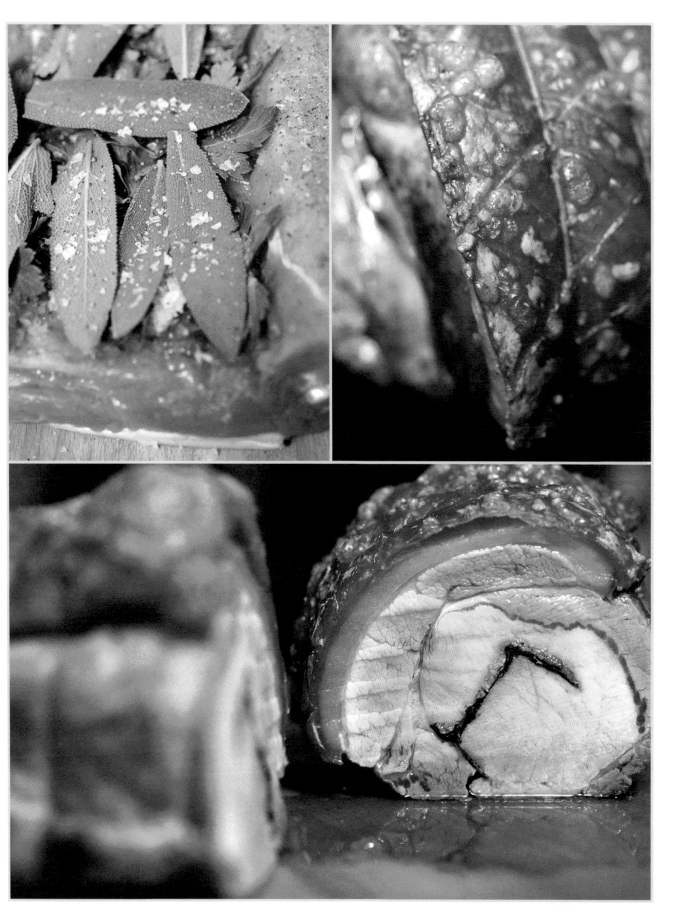

PRESSED BELLY OF PORK

66 Pork belly really needs long, slow-cooking to tenderise the meat. This recipe roasts the pork twice – first in a slow oven until the meat is fork tender, then in a very hot oven to produce a crispy and golden crackling. **99**

6–8 servings

1.3kg pork belly, ideally in one piece (see tip)
sea salt and freshly ground black pepper
olive oil, to drizzle
2 heads of garlic (unpeeled), halved horizontally
handful of thyme sprigs
splash of white wine
450ml Chicken stock (see page 246)

TIP If you buy pork belly from a supermarket, it will most likely be rolled. If so, remove the string and unroll. Lay flat on a board, skin side down, and cut a slit through the thick end of the pork to open it out like a butterfly so that the meat is evenly thick throughout.

Heat the oven to 170°C/Gas 3. Season the pork flesh with salt and pepper, then turn the pork belly over and score the skin with a sharp knife. Rub all over with olive oil, salt and pepper.

Place the garlic, halved side up, on a lightly oiled roasting tray and scatter over the thyme sprigs. Lay the pork belly on top, fat side up. Trickle with a little more olive oil and sprinkle with a little more sea salt. Add a splash of white wine, cover the tray with foil and bake for 1½ hours. Remove the foil, baste the pork with the juices and return to the oven, uncovered, for another ½–1 hour until tender. Continue to baste the pork occasionally with the pan juices.

Transfer the pork to a clean roasting tray to cool. Place another tray on top and weigh down with a tin to flatten the pork. Allow to cool and leave for several hours or overnight in the refrigerator to set the shape.

To make a gravy, skim off the excess fat from the roasting tray, then place on the hob over a medium heat. Deglaze with the chicken stock, scraping the bottom of the tray to release any sediment. Boil steadily until reduced and thickened.

Heat the oven to the highest setting, probably 240°C/Gas 9. Cut the pressed pork into individual portions or squares and pat the skin dry with kitchen paper. Place the pork squares, fat side up, in a roasting tray and drizzle with olive oil and a generous pinch of sea salt. Roast for 15 minutes until the skin is golden brown and crisp. Trim the sides of the pork pieces to neaten after roasting if you like.

Rest the pork for 5 minutes, then serve with the light gravy and accompaniments.

Caramelised apple wedges

Melt the butter in a wide non-stick frying pan. Dredge the apples in the caster sugar and add to the pan when the butter begins to foam. Fry for 3–4 minutes on each side over a medium heat until golden brown and caramelised. Toss in the spring onions and tarragon and serve warm.

6–8 servings

20g unsalted butter

3–4 Braeburn apples, cored, peeled and cut into wedges

50g caster sugar

1 spring onion, trimmed and finely sliced

few tarragon sprigs, leaves chopped

Broccoli with red onions, capers & almonds

6–8 servings

2 large heads of broccoli

2 tbsp olive oil, plus extra to drizzle

1 large red onion, peeled and roughly chopped

sea salt and freshly ground black pepper

2–3 tbsp red wine vinegar

2 tbsp capers, rinsed and drained

2 tbsp toasted flaked almonds (optional)

Cut the broccoli into florets. Trim away the fibrous skin from the stalks, then cut the tender core into small cubes. Heat the olive oil in a frying pan and cook the red onion over a medium heat, stirring occasionally, for 8–10 minutes until soft. Season with salt and pepper, deglaze the pan with the wine vinegar and cook for a few more minutes. Meanwhile, blanch the broccoli in boiling salted water for 2 minutes and drain well. Add to the onions along with the capers and a little more olive oil. Adjust the seasoning to taste. Serve warm with a scattering of flaked almonds if you like.

WHITE CHOCOLATE
PANNACOTTA WITH CHAMPAGNE GRANITA

" This may seem an unlikely combination, but the clean, crisp freshness of the granita really cuts through the richness of the white chocolate pannacotta. A great dessert for any season ... "

6–8 servings

CHAMPAGNE GRANITA:
125g caster sugar
3 tbsp liquid glucose
squeeze of lemon juice
250ml Champagne

PANNACOTTA:
600ml double cream
150ml milk
60g caster sugar
3 gelatine sheets
200g white chocolate, broken into
   small pieces

TO SERVE:
125g raspberries
finely pared lemon zest (optional)

First, make the granita. Put the sugar, 250ml water, the liquid glucose and lemon juice into a heavy-based pan and stir over a low heat until the sugar has dissolved. Increase the heat to high and let the sugar syrup bubble for 3 minutes. Leave to cool completely before adding the Champagne. Pour the mixture into a shallow plastic container and freeze for 2–3 hours until partially frozen. Scrape the semi-frozen granita with a fork and stir up the ice crystals. Return to the freezer until ready to use.

To make the pannacotta, put the cream, milk and sugar into a heavy-based saucepan over a low heat to melt the sugar, stirring occasionally. Meanwhile, soak the gelatine sheets in a shallow dish of cold water for a few minutes.

When the cream begins to bubble up the sides of the pan, take the pan off the heat. Stir in the white chocolate and continue to stir until it has melted. Squeeze the excess water from the gelatine leaves, add them to the warm mixture and stir well to dissolve. Pour the mixture into 6–8 darioles or other individual moulds. Stand the moulds on a tray and refrigerate for 5–6 hours or overnight until set. The pannacotta should still have a slight wobble when it is ready.

To turn out, dip the base of each dariole mould in a bowl of hot water for two seconds, then invert on to a small plate and give the mould a shake to release the pannacotta. Serve each pannacotta surrounded by raspberries and shavings of Champagne granita. Top with a curl of lemon zest if you like.

24 Paella for a crowd

This colourful menu captures some of the best Mediterranean flavours – slow-roasted plum tomatoes, fragrant basil and thyme, freshly marinated anchovies and a tempting array of shellfish in the paella. For a more indulgent dessert, serve Coffee & chocolate mousse cups (see page 147) to finish. This menu serves 8–10.

Roasted tomato salad with anchovies & prawns

Paella

Poached apricots with vanilla crème anglaise

planning your menu

THE DAY BEFORE...
• Prepare the poached apricots for the dessert and leave immersed in the syrup in the fridge overnight.
• Make the crème anglaise, cover the surface with cling film to prevent a skin forming and chill.
• Prepare the slow-roasted tomatoes for the salad.

AN HOUR AHEAD...
• Clean the shellfish and prepare the squid for the paella; keep chilled.

HALF AN HOUR AHEAD...
• For the starter, cook the prawns and prepare the other ingredients ready to assemble.
• Prepare all the ingredients for the paella, ready to cook.
• Cook the paella.

JUST BEFORE SERVING...
• Assemble the starter and serve.
• Leave the paella to stand, covered, while you eat the starter.
• Serve the paella straight from the pan.
• Plate the dessert and serve.

ROASTED TOMATO SALAD WITH ANCHOVIES & PRAWNS

" This gorgeous salad is full of punchy flavours. An ideal appetiser before paella, it also makes the perfect starter for an *al fresco* meal, or you can serve it as a side dish for a summer barbecue. Slow-roasting is an excellent way to bring out the flavour of tomatoes. I recommend you make double the quantity and save the extra for other dishes. Store the tomatoes in clean jars, covered with olive oil, in the fridge for up to 3 days. "

8–10 servings

SLOW-ROASTED TOMATOES:
18 plum tomatoes
olive oil, to drizzle
few thyme sprigs, leaves only
3 garlic cloves, peeled and thinly sliced
sea salt and freshly ground black pepper

SALAD:
300–400g tiger prawns, peeled and deveined
1 head of lollo rosso (or red oak lettuce), trimmed
large bunch of basil, leaves only
6–8 tbsp Classic vinaigrette (see page 247)
100g marinated anchovies (see tip)

TIP Freshly marinated anchovies are now available from the chilled delicatessen cabinet of selected supermarkets. Perfect for salads, they are less astringent than the salted and oiled options, which are better suited to cooked dishes.

For the tomatoes, heat the oven to its lowest setting, probably 100°C/Gas ¼. Cut the tomatoes in half lengthways. Drizzle a little olive oil over the bottom of a large shallow, ovenproof dish and scatter over the thyme leaves, garlic and a little salt and pepper. Arrange the tomatoes, cut side up, in a single layer over the thyme and garlic. Slowly roast in the oven for about an hour until the tomatoes are soft but still holding their shape. Leave to cool completely.

For the salad, bring a pan of salted water to the boil and reduce the heat to a simmer. Add the prawns and cook for 1–1½ minutes until they turn opaque. Refresh under cold running water and drain well.

Put the tomatoes into a large bowl. Tear the lettuce and basil leaves into pieces and add them to the bowl with the prawns. Toss the ingredients with the vinaigrette, then divide among serving plates. Garnish with the marinated anchovies and sprinkle with a little sea salt and black pepper to serve.

PAELLA

" To me, paella is the ultimate meal for an informal gathering of friends and family. Indeed, the Spanish have it as part of their Sunday lunch or supper. There are hundreds of variations available, with the common denomination being rice, saffron and olive oil. This highly flavoured version has a bit of everything, but you could pare it down and substitute a few ingredients if you like. "

8–10 servings

2 skinless and boneless chicken thighs, about 400g

4 tbsp olive oil, plus extra to drizzle

1 large Spanish onion, peeled and chopped

1 large red pepper, deseeded and chopped

3–4 garlic cloves, peeled and thinly sliced

2 long red chillies, sliced on the diagonal

few thyme sprigs

sea salt and freshly ground black pepper

200g chorizo sausage, sliced

1 tsp paprika

500g paella rice (or long-grain rice)

splash of dry sherry

½ tsp saffron strands

4 large tomatoes, roughly chopped

500g fresh clams, cleaned (see page 59)

300g raw king prawns (whole or heads removed)

300g squid, cleaned and sliced into thin rings

400g peas (thawed, if frozen)

Put the kettle on to boil. Cut the chicken into bite-sized pieces. Heat a splash of olive oil in a large paella pan. Add the onion, red pepper, garlic, chillies and thyme, and sauté over a high heat for a few minutes until the vegetables start to soften. Season the chicken with salt and pepper, then add to the pan along with the chorizo and paprika. Fry, stirring frequently, over a high heat for to lightly seal the meat.

Tip in the rice and stir for 2–3 minutes, then add a good splash of sherry and pour in enough boiling water to cover the rice by about 1cm. Bring to a simmer and sprinkle in the saffron strands, stirring well to distribute them. Add the tomatoes and season well with salt and pepper. Allow to simmer, stirring frequently, for about 10–12 minutes.

Add the clams and prawns, with a little more boiling water if needed, and stir through. Cook over a medium heat for 3 minutes until the prawns are opaque and the clams start to open up. Finally, stir in the squid and peas. The squid should only take 1–2 minutes to cook – it will turn opaque when it is ready. Taste and adjust the seasoning.

Take the pan off the heat, cover with foil and leave to stand for 5 minutes to allow the flavours to meld together. Drizzle a little olive oil over the paella and bring the pan to the table to serve.

POACHED APRICOTS
WITH VANILLA CRÈME ANGLAISE

" Ripe fresh apricots are poached in a sugar syrup infused with aromatics to bring out their flavour. You can poach the fruit a day ahead and keep it in the fridge. Save the leftover syrup in a jar, ready to drizzle over vanilla ice cream or fruit salads. "

8–10 servings

750ml Sugar syrup (see page 248)
1 vanilla pod
1 cinnamon stick
1 lemongrass stalk, split lengthways
1 tsp coriander seeds
1 tsp black peppercorns
16–20 just ripe fresh apricots
1 quantity Crème anglaise (see page 248)

Pour the sugar syrup into a shallow, wide pan. Split the vanilla pod and scrape out the seeds with the back of a knife, adding them to the pan along with the vanilla pod, cinnamon, lemongrass, coriander seeds and peppercorns. Bring to a simmer.

Add half the apricots and poach for about 10–15 minutes until tender but not oversoft, carefully turning several times during cooking. Remove with a slotted spoon to a large plate. Add the rest of the apricots to the sugar syrup and poach in the same way, then transfer to the plate and leave until cool enough to handle.

Strain the syrup through a sieve into a large bowl. Peel off the skins from the apricots, then cut in half and discard the stones. Immerse the apricots in the sugar syrup, cover the bowl with cling film and chill for at least 3 hours or overnight.

Arrange the apricots on wide plates and drizzle with a little of their aromatic syrup. Pour the crème anglaise around the fruit and serve.

Summer entertaining

A sumptuous summer spread centred around a freshly baked salmon with gorgeous accompaniments. I start the meal with a selection of interesting little appetisers and finish with hot soufflés that taste as amazing as they look. Follow my step-by-step guide to preparing this meal on the accompanying DVD. This menu serves 6–8.

Antipasti:

+ Stuffed courgette rolls   + Balsamic beetroot with Roquefort

+ Parma ham, sage & Parmesan puffs   + Marinated mushrooms

Salmon baked with herbs & caramelised lemons

+ Pink grapefruit hollandaise

+ Cos, red onion & asparagus salad   + Minted new potatoes (see page 191)

Passion fruit & banana soufflé

planning your menu

A FEW DAYS AHEAD...
• Order the whole salmon from your fishmonger (arranging to collect it a day ahead, or on the day if possible).

SEVERAL HOURS IN ADVANCE
• For the antipasti, prepare the marinated mushrooms and balsamic beetroot; keep both chilled.

TWO HOURS AHEAD...
• Make the crème pâtissière base for the soufflé; leave to cool. Prepare the soufflé dishes.
• Scrub the potatoes and immerse in cold water.
• Make the choux paste for the puffs; leave to cool.

AN HOUR OR SO AHEAD...
• Prepare the courgette strips and filling ready to assemble; chill.
• Prepare the salad, ready to assemble.
• Add the fruit purée and passion fruit juice to the soufflé base.
• Make and bake the Parmesan puffs (or do so earlier and keep warm).
• Prepare the salmon ready for baking.
• Prepare the hollandaise; keep warm.
• Assemble the courgette rolls.

JUST BEFORE SERVING...
• Assemble the antipasti and serve.
• Bake the salmon and cook the potatoes while you eat the starter.
• Leave the salmon to rest while you dress the potatoes and assemble the salad. Serve the main course.
• Finish the soufflés, bake and serve immediately.

ANTIPASTI

" I love the way Italians start a meal with a platter of tempting foods to tantalise the palate. This is my take on antipasti – a selection of interesting warm and cold bites that can be prepared in advance. "

Stuffed courgette rolls

6–8 servings

4 small courgettes, trimmed
olive oil, to oil and drizzle
250g ricotta
juice of ½ lemon
splash of extra virgin olive oil
sea salt and freshly ground black
  pepper
handful of basil leaves, chopped
50g pine nuts, toasted
balsamic vinegar, to drizzle

Slice the courgettes lengthways, using a swivel vegetable peeler or a mandolin and select about 40 good strips. Place the courgette strips on an oiled tray and brush with olive oil. Season with salt and pepper and chill for 20 minutes.

Mix the ricotta with the lemon juice, extra virgin olive oil and seasoning to taste, then fold in the chopped basil and pine nuts. Place a small teaspoonful of ricotta mixture on one end of a courgette strip and roll up. Repeat to use up all the filling. Arrange the courgette cannelloni on a plate and grind over some black pepper. Drizzle with a little olive oil and balsamic vinegar and serve.

Balsamic beetroot with Roquefort

6–8 servings

600g cooked baby beetroot, peeled
3–4 tbsp olive oil
6–7 tbsp balsamic vinegar
sea salt and freshly ground black pepper
150g Roquefort
1–2 tsp sesame seeds, toasted

Halve the beetroot or quarter, depending on size. Heat the olive oil in a large sauté pan, add the beetroot and sauté for 2–3 minutes. Add the balsamic vinegar and season with salt and pepper. Toss to coat the beetroot in the syrupy glaze. Transfer to a bowl, leave to cool completely, then chill for a few hours.

Crumble the Roquefort over the beetroot and sprinkle with toasted sesame seeds to serve.

Parma ham, sage & Parmesan puffs

Heat the oven to 200°C/Gas 6. Put the butter and 220ml water into a heavy-based saucepan. Heat slowly to melt the butter, then turn up the heat and bring to a rolling boil. Meanwhile, sift the flour and salt together. As soon as the liquid comes up to a boil, tip in all the flour and salt and take the pan off the heat. Beat vigorously with a wooden spoon until the mixture comes together as a paste and leaves the sides of the pan. Spread on a plate and leave to cool.

Return the paste to the pan (or place in a bowl) and beat in the eggs, a little at a time, until soft, shiny and smooth. The mixture should have a dropping consistency (you may not need all of the egg). Beat in the chopped Parma ham, sage and Parmesan until evenly incorporated. Lightly grease a large baking sheet. Spoon the mixture into a piping bag fitted with a 1–1.5cm plain nozzle and pipe into small 3–4cm rounds on the baking sheet, spacing them about 5cm apart to leave room for expansion. Bake for 20–25 minutes or until the pastries are well risen and golden brown. Serve immediately or keep warm in a low oven.

Makes about 35

85g unsalted butter, plus extra to grease
100g plain flour
pinch of salt
3 medium eggs, beaten
100g Parma ham, finely chopped
4–5 sage leaves, finely shredded
40g Parmesan, finely grated

Marinated mushrooms

Heat the olive oil in a large wide heavy-based pan. When it is almost smoking, add the mushrooms and sauté over a high heat for about 5 minutes until they are lightly golden. Tip in the shallots and season well with salt and pepper. Sauté until the shallots have softened. Add a splash of wine vinegar and let the liquid bubble for a few minutes. Drizzle generously with olive oil and allow to cool to room temperature. Sprinkle with tarragon to serve.

6–8 servings

4–5 tbsp olive oil, plus extra to drizzle
500g button mushrooms, cleaned, trimmed and halved if large
2–3 shallots, peeled and sliced
sea salt and freshly ground black pepper
generous splash of white wine vinegar
small bunch of tarragon, leaves only

239

SALMON BAKED WITH HERBS & CARAMELISED LEMONS

" The delicate flavour of salmon really comes through when it is oven-steamed on a bed of herbs. The juice of the caramelised lemons further enhances the fish. You can serve the salmon simply with its cooking juices or elevate the dish to another level by serving it with a gorgeous Pink grapefruit hollandaise (see page 243). **"**

6–8 servings

1 whole salmon, about 1.6 kg, scaled, gutted and washed
olive oil, for cooking and to drizzle
sea salt and freshly ground black pepper
2 bay leaves
few sprigs each of rosemary, thyme, basil, sage and parsley
1 head of garlic (unpeeled), halved horizontally, then broken into cloves
2–3 lemongrass stalks, split in half lengthways and bruised with the back of a knife
1 large or 3 small lemons, thickly sliced
5–6 star anise
1 tsp mixed (or black) peppercorns

Trim a little off the tail and fins of the salmon with kitchen scissors and pat dry with kitchen paper. Pat the cavity dry as well. Score the skin of the salmon on both sides with a sharp knife, at 1–2 cm intervals. Rub all over with olive oil, salt and pepper.

Tear two sheets of foil, large enough to envelope the salmon easily. Lay one on top of the other on the work surface and scatter the bay leaves, herb sprigs, garlic and lemongrass over the middle of the foil. Lay the fish on the bed of herbs and tuck some of the flavourings into the cavity.

Fry the lemon slices in a little olive oil for 2–3 minutes until caramelised around the edges, seasoning them with salt and pepper. Allow to cool slightly. Tuck the caramelised lemon slices around the fish, placing some in the cavity and some on top. Scatter the star anise and peppercorns over and around the fish, putting some inside the cavity. Drizzle the salmon with a little olive oil. Heat the oven to 190°C/Gas 5.

Fold the edges of the foil tightly together over the salmon to seal, leaving some space in the parcel for steam to surround and cook the fish. Put the salmon parcel in the roasting tin and cook in the centre of the oven for 25–30 minutes, depending on the thickness of the salmon. Remove from the oven and without unwrapping the foil parcel, rest the fish for 5–10 minutes.

Unwrap the salmon and peel off the skin with a palette knife. Use the back of a spoon to slide the fish off the bone. Serve individual portions garnished with the caramelised lemons and accompanied by the pink grapefruit hollandaise and salad.

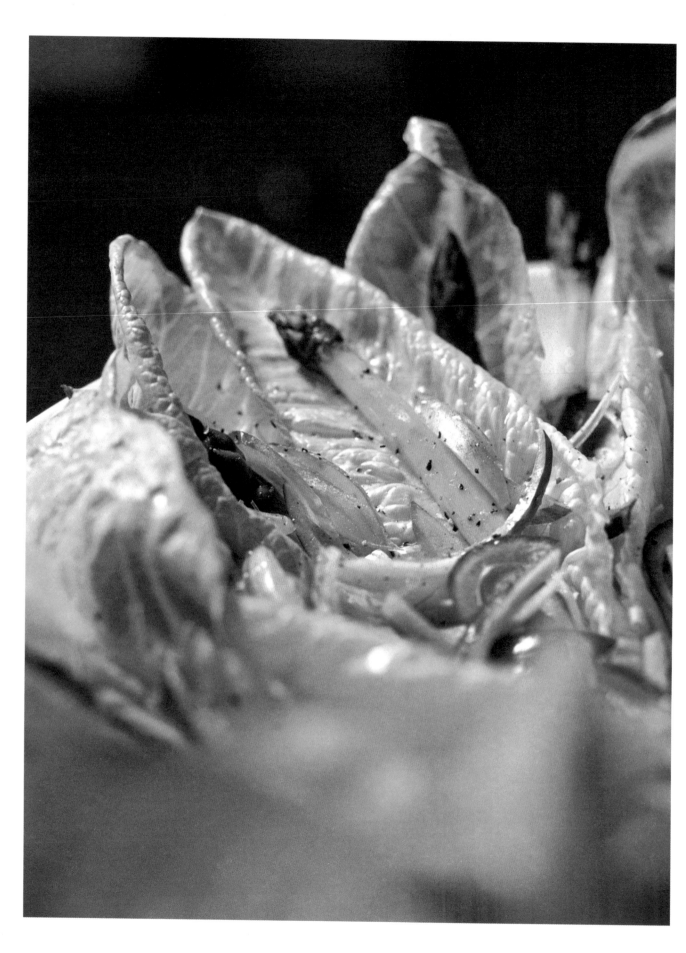

Pink grapefruit hollandaise

Put the egg yolks, grapefruit zest and juice, coriander and 1 tbsp warm water into a heatproof bowl and set over a pan of simmering water. Whisk, using a balloon whisk, until the mixture is pale, creamy and falls in a slow ribbon. Remove the bowl from the heat and whisk for a further 3 minutes until the mixture has cooled slightly. Whisk in 1 tbsp olive oil, then gradually whisk in the rest in a thin steady stream until it is all incorporated and the sauce is a good coating consistency. Season with salt and pepper to taste and add a little extra grapefruit juice if you think it needs it. If the sauce is a little too thick, stir in a tiny splash of warm water. Keep warm in a bain-marie (or bowl over hot water) until ready to serve.

Makes about 300ml

3 egg yolks
finely grated zest of 1 pink grapefruit
juice of ½ pink grapefruit, plus an extra
squeeze to taste
6–8 coriander seeds, finely crushed
150ml light olive oil
sea salt and freshly ground white pepper

Cos, red onion & asparagus salad

6–8 servings

300g asparagus spears, trimmed and
stalks peeled
sea salt and freshly ground black pepper
2 large cos lettuce, washed
1 red onion, peeled and thinly sliced
3–4 tbsp Classic vinaigrette (see page 247)

Blanch the asparagus in a pan of boiling salted water for 1½–2 minutes until just tender. Drain and refresh under cold running water. Trim off the base of the lettuces and arrange the leaves over a large serving bowl. Put a blanched asparagus spear into the centre of each lettuce leaf and scatter over the sliced onions. Sprinkle with salt and pepper and drizzle with a little vinaigrette just before serving.

PASSION FRUIT & BANANA SOUFFLÉ

66 This is a soufflé that Angela Hartnett serves at the Connaught and it is amazingly good. The banana and passion fruit marry perfectly, giving the soufflé an extraordinary, delicate and subtle flavour. 99

Makes 6–8

CRÈME PATISSIÈRE BASE:
150ml milk
100ml double cream
15g plain flour
10g cornflour
3 large egg yolks
50g caster sugar

SOUFFLÉ:
4 ripe passion fruit
1 banana, about 100g, peeled
squeeze of lemon juice
2 tbsp banana liqueur (optional)
about 20g butter, melted, to brush
50g caster sugar, plus extra to dust
grated chocolate, to dust (optional)
2 large egg whites
icing sugar, to dust

TIP Don't be tempted to open the oven door until the soufflés are almost ready or they may collapse.

For the crème patissière
base, heat the milk and cream in a heavy-based saucepan until almost boiling. Sift the flour and cornflour together. Beat the egg yolks and sugar together in a large bowl, then mix in the flour. Add a splash of the hot creamy milk and whisk well until the mixture is smooth, then gradually whisk in the rest of the milk. Pour back into the pan and whisk over a medium-low heat for 3–5 minutes until thickened and smooth. Transfer to a bowl, cover and cool to room temperature, stirring occasionally to prevent a skin forming.

Halve the passion fruit
and scoop out the seeds and juice into a sieve set over a bowl. Press to extract the juice, then pour into a blender. Break the banana into pieces and add to the blender with the lemon juice and liqueur if using. Whiz until smooth, then stir this mixture into the crème patissière and set aside.

Heat the oven
to 190°C/Gas 5. Brush 6–8 deep ramekins with a generous layer of melted butter, using upward strokes. Dust the insides either with caster sugar or grated chocolate (or coat some with each) and chill to set.

When ready to serve,
whisk the egg whites in a clean bowl to firm peaks, then gradually whisk in the 50g caster sugar a spoonful at a time to make a firm, glossy meringue. Whisk a third of the meringue into the the crème patissière base, then very carefully fold in the rest, using a large metal spoon.

Divide the soufflé mix
among the prepared dishes and tap them on the work surface to level the mixture. Smooth the tops with a palette knife, then run the knife around the edge. (This helps the soufflés to rise evenly.) Sit the ramekins on a wide baking tray and bake for 10–12 minutes until well risen and lightly golden on top. The soufflés should wobble gently in the middle when ready. Dust with icing sugar and serve at once.

BASICS

Chicken stock
Makes about 1.5 litres

Put 1 chopped carrot, 1 chopped onion, 2 sliced celery stalks and 1 sliced leek in a large pan with 2 tbsp olive oil and cook over a medium heat until golden. Add a sprig of thyme, 1 bay leaf, 3 peeled garlic cloves, 2 tbsp tomato purée and 2 tbsp plain flour and cook, stirring, for a few minutes. Add 1kg raw chicken bones, cover with plenty of cold water and season lightly. Bring to the boil and skim. Simmer for 1 hour and then pass through a chinois or fine sieve. Adjust the seasoning.

Brown chicken stock This is used for a greater depth of flavour.
Follow the above recipe, roasting the chicken bones at 200°C/Gas 6 for 20 minutes before adding them. Brown duck stock can be made in the same way.

Fish stock
Makes about 1 litre

This is quick to make, using fish trimmings, or you can use crab or lobster shells. Heat 2 tbsp olive oil in a large pan. Add ½ chopped onion, ½ sliced celery stalk and 1 chopped fennel slice, and cook until soft but not coloured. Add 1kg fish trimmings (white fish bones and heads), a glass of white wine and enough water to cover. Bring to the boil, season lightly and simmer for 20 minutes. Pass through a chinois or fine sieve and adjust the seasoning.

TIP Make up these stocks in batches and keep them in the fridge (for up to 5 days) or freezer (up to 3 months) until required.

Court bouillon
Makes about 1 litre

A poaching liquor used for cooking whole fish and shellfish, such as lobster and crab. Place 1 chopped carrot, 1 chopped onion, a few bay leaves, 1 tsp black peppercorns, 1 tsp rock salt and 100ml white wine vinegar in a large pan and pour in 800ml water. Bring to the boil, then let it simmer for 20–30 minutes. Strain through a fine sieve and use immediately or cool and keep in the fridge for up to 3 days.

Velouté
Makes about 500ml

Heat a knob of butter in a wide saucepan. Stir in 3 finely chopped shallots and sauté gently for about 10 minutes until soft but not coloured. Pour in 200ml dry white wine and 200ml dry vermouth and boil until reduced by half. Then add 400ml stock (fish, vegetable or chicken), return to the boil and reduce by half. Stir in 300ml double cream and simmer gently until the sauce is the consistency of pouring cream. Season to taste with salt and pepper and strain the sauce through a fine sieve.

Classic vinaigrette
Makes about 250ml

Put 100ml extra virgin olive oil, 100ml groundnut oil, 1 scant tsp Dijon mustard, 1 tbsp lemon juice, 2 tbsp white wine vinegar and some sea salt and pepper in a measuring jug and whisk together until emulsified. Pour into a clean bottle, seal and refrigerate. Shake well before using.

Mayonnaise
Makes about 300ml

In a mixing bowl, whisk together 2 large egg yolks, 1 tsp white wine vinegar, 1 tsp English mustard and a pinch of sea salt. Slowly add 300ml groundnut oil, drop by drop to begin with, then in a thin stream, whisking constantly until thick and emulsified. (If the mayonnaise splits, mix another egg yolk with a pinch of seasoning and a little mustard and slowly whisk in the split mixture. It should re-emulsify). Season with salt and pepper to taste and chill. Use within 3 days.

Crème anglaise
Makes about 1.2 litres

Heat 500ml whole milk, 500ml double cream and 1 tbsp sugar in a heavy-based saucepan. Scrape the seeds from 2 split vanilla pods and add to the pan. In a large bowl, beat together 12 egg yolks and 85g caster sugar. As soon as the milk and cream begin to boil, take the pan off the heat. Gradually pour the hot liquid on to the sugary yolks, whisking continuously. Strain the mixture through a sieve into a clean pan. Stir the mixture over a low heat until the custard thickens enough to thinly coat the back of a spoon. Remove the pan from the heat and strain the custard again through a fine sieve. Leave to cool, stirring occasionally to prevent a skin forming.

Sugar syrup
Makes about 750ml

Put 250g caster sugar, 500ml water and the finely pared zest of ½ lemon into a heavy-based saucepan. Bring slowly to the boil, stirring to help dissolve the sugar. Bring the syrup to the boil and let it bubble for 5 minutes. Cool completely then transfer to a sealed container and refrigerate, unless using immediately.

French meringue nests
Makes about 8–10

These are the perfect base for serving soft fruits with whipped cream or ice cream. Heat the oven to the lowest setting, 100°C/Gas ¼. Using a hand-held electric beater, whisk 2 large egg whites in a clean, grease-free bowl with a pinch of salt until the egg whites hold firm peaks. Gradually whisk in 100g caster sugar, 1 tbsp at a time. Continue to whisk until the meringue is glossy and holds its shape. Spoon or pipe the meringue into round discs, about 2cm thick, on a lined baking tray. Bake for at least 2 hours until slightly crusty on top, then turn off the heat and let the meringues dry out in the oven for 6 hours or overnight. Peel the meringues off the baking parchment and store in an airtight container for up to a week.

Shortcrust pastry
Makes 375g

Sift 225g plain flour and 1 tsp salt into a food processor. Add 140g cold unsalted butter, in small pieces, and whiz for 10 seconds until the mixture resembles coarse breadcrumbs, then tip into a mixing bowl. Pour in 4 tbsp of ice cold water and stir the mixture with a knife until the dough comes together. Add another 1 tbsp water if it seems too dry. (Don't make it too wet, as a crumbly pastry results in a lighter crust.) Press the mixture into a dough, wrap in cling film and chill for at least 30 minutes before using.

Sweet flan pastry
Makes about 500g

Put 125g unsalted butter (at room temperature) and 90g caster sugar in a food processor and whiz until just combined. Add a large egg and whiz for 30 seconds. Tip in 250g plain flour and process for a few seconds until the dough just comes together. (Be careful not to over-process or the dough will become tough.) Add 1 tbsp cold water if the dough seems too dry. Knead lightly on a floured surface, then shape into a flat disc, wrap in cling film and chill for 30 minutes before rolling out.

Crêpes
Makes 6–7 crêpes

Sift 100g plain flour and ¼ tsp fine sea salt into a large bowl and make a well in the centre. Beat 1 large egg and 200ml milk together and pour into the well. Gradually whisk the flour into the wet mixture until the batter is well combined and smooth. Let the batter stand for 20 minutes. Heat a non-stick crêpe pan with a knob of butter. Give the batter a stir and pour a small ladleful into the pan. Quickly swirl the batter around the pan, pouring off any excess, and cook until golden brown at the edges. Flip the crêpe to cook the other side for 30 seconds. Repeat until all the batter has been used.

Herb crêpes
Add 2 tbsp of chopped mixed herbs, such as parsley, tarragon, chervil and chives, to the egg and milk mixture, then whisk into the flour. Continue as for basic crêpes.

INDEX

ACKNOWLEDGEMENTS

A book of this quality can only be put together with the strength and dedication of the talented team that I am so lucky to be working with. Once again, I am indebted to my 'adopted son', Mark Sargeant, who has worked tirelessly on every photo shoot and always manages to lighten the day with his humour. Mark now leaves the family to get married, but remains my right-hand man. I am very grateful to Pat Llewellyn and everyone at Optomen TV for helping me with the incredible Sunday lunch campaign. Pat and I work together almost like tomato and basil in the kitchen. And I owe a special thanks to my dear Emily, for her hard work, patience and understanding of what precious time I have. Dynamic meetings with her left me enough time to play football ... brilliant, Emily.

A big thank you to Helen Lewis, as always. Helen helped me with my first ever book, so she has been there from the start and knows me inside out, which is apparent throughout this book. I now regard her as an integral member of our kitchen brigade. And to the newly found yummy mummy of the photography world, Jill, who is terrific. Her enthusiasm is infectious, though I cringe when she calls me poppet! And Janet Illsley, for being forever demanding and scrutinising editorial-wise, a job well done yet again...I think I owe you twelve dinners now, twelve tables for two. And, of course, Anne Furniss and Alison Cathie, for trusting the vision to get behind this campaign.

And thanks to everyone at Gordon Ramsay Holdings, from Gillian Thomson to Chris Hutcheson. Also to Jo Barnes for her strategy and determination to make this book a big hit. And to Tony Turnbull from The Times who has shared my passion for the Sunday lunch campaign from day one. Without all these people listed, this book wouldn't f...... be here!

And finally to my four new sous chefs Jack, Holly, Megan, and Matilda. A huge thanks for tasting all the recipes that your father is cooking ... and under no circumstances do you send any of his food back. Thanks, also, to my mother, Helen, for being a great prop... you may not like having your picture taken Mum, but you look terrific! And last but not least, to the most patient woman in Britain today, my beloved wife Tana.

Editorial director **Anne Furniss**
Art director **Helen Lewis**
Project editor **Janet Illsley**
Photographer **Jill Mead**
Food stylist **Mark Sargeant**
Home economist **Emily Quah**
Assistant designer **Katherine Case**
Editorial assistant **Andrew Bayliss**
Production **Vincent Smith, Ruth Deary**

Optomen Television Production Consultants:
Patricia Llewellyn (Managing director); Eileen Herlihy (Series producer); Sarah Wood (Producer); Sarah Durdin-Robertson (Assistant producer, food)

Optomen Television Limited
1, Valentine Place
London SE1 8QH
www.optomen.com

optomen
television

First published in 2006 by
Quadrille Publishing Limited
Alhambra House, 27-31 Charing Cross Road, London WC2H 0LS
www.quadrille.co.uk

Text © 2006 Gordon Ramsay
Photography © 2006 Jill Mead
Design and layout © 2006 Quadrille Publishing Limited
Format and programme © 2006 Optomen Television Limited

Cataloguing in Publication Data: a catalogue record for this book is available from the British Library.

ISBN (978) 184400 280 2 (1)

Printed in Italy

All survey statistics used in this book are derived from the F Word/Gfk NOP Survey, February 2006.

ACKNOWLEDGEMENTS

A book of this quality can only be put together with the strength and dedication of the talented team that I am so lucky to be working with. Once again, I am indebted to my 'adopted son', Mark Sargeant, who has worked tirelessly on every photo shoot and always manages to lighten the day with his humour. Mark now leaves the family to get married, but remains my right-hand man. I am very grateful to Pat Llewellyn and everyone at Optomen TV for helping me with the incredible Sunday lunch campaign. Pat and I work together almost like tomato and basil in the kitchen. And I owe a special thanks to my dear Emily, for her hard work, patience and understanding of what precious time I have. Dynamic meetings with her left me enough time to play football ... brilliant, Emily.

A big thank you to Helen Lewis, as always. Helen helped me with my first ever book, so she has been there from the start and knows me inside out, which is apparent throughout this book. I now regard her as an integral member of our kitchen brigade. And to the newly found yummy mummy of the photography world, Jill, who is terrific. Her enthusiasm is infectious, though I cringe when she calls me poppet! And Janet Illsley, for being forever demanding and scrutinising editorial-wise, a job well done yet again...I think I owe you twelve dinners now, twelve tables for two. And, of course, Anne Furniss and Alison Cathie, for trusting the vision to get behind this campaign.

And thanks to everyone at Gordon Ramsay Holdings, from Gillian Thomson to Chris Hutcheson. Also to Jo Barnes for her strategy and determination to make this book a big hit. And to Tony Turnbull from The Times who has shared my passion for the Sunday lunch campaign from day one. Without all these people listed, this book wouldn't f...... be here!

And finally to my four new sous chefs Jack, Holly, Megan, and Matilda. A huge thanks for tasting all the recipes that your father is cooking ... and under no circumstances do you send any of his food back. Thanks, also, to my mother, Helen, for being a great prop... you may not like having your picture taken Mum, but you look terrific! And last but not least, to the most patient woman in Britain today, my beloved wife Tana.

Editorial director **Anne Furniss**
Art director **Helen Lewis**
Project editor **Janet Illsley**
Photographer **Jill Mead**
Food stylist **Mark Sargeant**
Home economist **Emily Quah**
Assistant designer **Katherine Case**
Editorial assistant **Andrew Bayliss**
Production **Vincent Smith, Ruth Deary**

Optomen Television Production Consultants:
Patricia Llewellyn (Managing director); Eileen Herlihy (Series producer); Sarah Wood (Producer); Sarah Durdin-Robertson (Assistant producer, food)

Optomen Television Limited
1, Valentine Place
London SE1 8QH
www.optomen.com
optomen television

First published in 2006 by
Quadrille Publishing Limited
Alhambra House, 27-31 Charing Cross Road, London WC2H 0LS
www.quadrille.co.uk

Text © 2006 Gordon Ramsay
Photography © 2006 Jill Mead
Design and layout © 2006 Quadrille Publishing Limited
Format and programme © 2006 Optomen Television Limited

Cataloguing in Publication Data: a catalogue record for this book is available from the British Library.

ISBN (978) 184400 280 2 (1)

Printed in Italy

All survey statistics used in this book are derived from the F Word/Gfk NOP Survey, February 2006.